TWAYNE'S WORLD AUTHORS SERIES

A Survey of the World's Literature

Sylvia E. Bowman, Indiana University
GENERAL EDITOR

GREECE

Mary P. Gianos, Detroit Institute of Technology
EDITOR

Epicurus

(TWAS 17)

TWAYNE'S WORLD AUTHORS SERIES (TWAS)

The purpose of TWAS is to survey the major writers —novelists, dramatists, historians, poets, philosophers, and critics—of the nations of the world. Among the national literatures covered are those of Australia, Canada, China, Eastern Europe, France, Germany, Greece, India, Italy, Japan, Latin America, New Zealand, Poland, Russia, Scandinavia, Spain, and the African nations, as well as Hebrew, Yiddish, and Latin Classical literatures. This survey is complemented by Twayne's United States Authors Series and English Authors Series.

The intent of each volume in these series is to present a critical-analytical study of the works of the writer; to include biographical and historical material that may be necessary for understanding, appreciation, and critical appraisal of the writer; and to present all material in clear, concise English—but not to vitiate the scholarly content of the work by doing so.

Epicurus

By GEORGE A. PANICHAS

University of Maryland

Twayne Publishers, Inc. :: New York

28524

Preface

To introduce the general reader to the philosophy of Epicurus is the central purpose of this book. Essentially, therefore, this volume could be described as an introductory essay, beyond which it has no pretensions.

In an age when the degree of specialization reaches dangerous proportions, even in the humanities, the need to communicate with the general reader is doubly urgent. No doubt, some persons will regard the desire to communicate with the nonspecialist reader as a kind of popularization of scholarship, conducive to a leveling process. This view, however, must be seen as constituting a form of academic parochialism, no less insidious and no less threatening than an ascending faith in the expanding technocracy of modern civilization.

As K. R. Popper notes in his valuable study *The Open Society and Its Enemies,* the conflict is relentless between the forces speaking for an "open society," which seeks to free the critical faculties of man, and the forces advocating a "closed society," which submits to magical and arbitrary powers. If the struggle against the totalitarian mentality is to succeed, it cannot do so in a society that stifles the exchange of ideas or in any way fears attempts to bring ideological issues to the attention of readers who are not necessarily experts. By no means does the need for general studies lessen the worth of the specialist scholar. Without his contributions a volume such as this would be impossible to write. What it does mean is that the study of philosophy cannot and must not be confined to an area of pure specialisms, for philosophy has the whole of the world and all of mankind as its province.

If a subtitle amplifying the aim of this book were to be given, "A Primer of Nonconformity" would be entirely appropriate. For throughout, Epicurus is treated as a nonconformist thinker and teacher. And his nonconformity, it will be seen, is closely linked with the never-ending struggle between the "open society" and the "closed society." As such, this incessant struggle has particular importance and makes particular demands and imposes particular tests on those persons who are concerned with the survival of humaneness, reasonableness, and freedom in civilization.

Epicurus' own words, "I was never anxious to please the mob. I had never learnt the sort of thing they liked, and the things I knew were far removed from their perception," epitomize the impelling nature of his dissent and could serve as an epigraph to the whole of his life and thought. In the founding of his school in Athens; in his concepts of the atom and of the universe; in his feelings toward politics, toward education, toward organized religion, toward the gods, and toward death; in his treatment of the soul; in his views on ethics, on morals, on pleasure, and on happiness; and in his veneration of friendship between man and man and between man and woman, Epicurus exemplifies the strengths of nonconformity. The significance of his nonconformity must not go unnoticed: In resisting those who would enforce a "closed society," with its autocratic ways, its militarism, its contempt for sensitive spirit, Epicurus and his followers affirmed a faith not only in man's intelligence and dignity but also in an enlightened vision of the universe and of man's place in that universe.

In so far as Epicurus' nonconformity was of an extraordinary kind, it needs to be seen in a different context from the usual dimensions of nonconformity. That is to say, it was not the nonconformity that we are accustomed to associate with mass meetings, with long protest marches, with clamorous speeches, with self-inflicted death. Epicurus' temper of dissent and his holding to unpopular opinions were ultimately connected with a higher and more refined nonconformity. Vigorous, yet not violent; dogmatic, yet not coercive; uncompromising, yet not insensitive, it can perhaps be described as a marginal nonconformity: one that seeks for a manageable solitude and that refuses to conform to the outer world of organization, power, and materiality in order to secure the harmony and peace of the inner life. Yet, Epicurean nonconformity must not be viewed as being effete or immoderately esthetic. Side by side with its inspired vision of serenity are its stringent criticisms of the religious, social, economic, and political structures of society.

Precisely because of its delicacy and its nonviolence, Epicurus' nonconformity, like his philosophical doctrine in general, has been misunderstood and misrepresented. Thus, for instance, in an issue of *The Quarterly Review* published in London in 1897, there appeared a long, unsigned essay, "Epicurus and His Sayings." On the whole, this essay is a welcome and judicious defense of Epicurus' thought. But in parts it also typifies an attitude that inheres in recurrent criticisms of Epicureanism. First of all, this attitude is critical of Epicurus for being passive and for glorifying "a lifetime of mere safety and quiet," or in the words of *The Quarterly Review:* "Those who are vigorous in body and manly in character do not construct a philosophy of life with the special motive of escaping the strain of anxiety, danger, or toil." And second, it is critical of Epicurus because his teachings betray the spirit of adventure. To quote again: "He seems not to have known that there is a pleasure to human nature in doing a difficult thing, that hard lives are often happy ones, and to a pure and healthy mind are more satisfying than ease and quiet, and that to many men danger and hardship combined are enticing."

Indifference, passivity, withdrawal, and lack of energy: these, it is often claimed, are the crippling weaknesses emerging from Epicurus' doctrines. A curiously revealing claim, it reflects an insistence on tangible accomplishments and on the virtues of activism. Increasingly, and painfully, it becomes evident that Western civilization has been conditioned to assess the whole meaning of life, of history itself, according to measurable functions and values.

Epicurus, of course, asserted the ultimate meaningfulness of the secular life. But it is a delicate, ennobling secularism that he preached, transcending all that is blatant and vulgar. How to free man from being a slave to the things of this world or to the dreams of the heavenly world is the crucial, the testing problem which Epicurus attempted to solve. In a sense, therefore, he was seeking for man's total liberation both from the oppressiveness of mortality and from the illusion of immortality.

The Epicurean wise man is ever aware of the follies of both these realms and strives to find a balance in a realm that stands midway between the eternal tensions of the physical and the metaphysical. "We have to know how to go out and meet one another upon the third ground, the holy ground." These words, written by a famous modern nonconformist, the English novelist D. H. Lawrence—though they are words that could just as easily have been written by Epicurus—are particularly pertinent at this point: It is on this "third ground, the holy ground," that Epicurus communed with his followers, attaining here the reverence for life and the life of dialogue which this world often spurns and which the world beyond immobilizes.

If a modern reader is to appreciate Epicurus' doctrine and the peculiar nature of his nonconformity, he must realize that it is the quiet life that, for the ancient philosopher, embodied the good life: a life that ultimately achieves not only a release from pain and anxiety but also an intelligent and sustaining faith. Epicurus' rejection of his social milieu grew out of a profound need to see life from another angle of vision. As such his nonconformity was of the most humanizing kind, for it addressed itself to the inner condition of man, not to man's exterior concerns—in short, to man's health, not to man's salvation.

Epicurus' purpose, hence, was to purify *this* life of dissonance and to overcome the directives of religious, philosophical, and political masters—the Platos, the Aristotles, the Alexanders—which in the end lead, he believed, to much needless anguish and pain. That at first Epicureanism attracted many followers, and that, above all, it secured this success by peaceful persuasion, attests to the genius and the worth of a philosopher who affirmed man's capacity for self-mastery. Epicurus' garden is symbolic of what man can do to live the good life. Indeed, the Epicurean garden signifies the way of tranquillity as opposed to the way of struggle.

No one can study the many and various writings of philosophers and literary artists in the twentieth century—the "Terrible Twentieth," as it has been called—without sensing a desperate desire for the feeling of community and for the serenity which Epicurus considered to be healing powers which help man to live harmoniously. When a philosopher like the late Martin Buber depicts the modern world as a "depersonalized society" in which "atrophy of personal existence" and "social and cosmic homelessness" are manifest, Epicurus' doctrines assume a wisdom of timeless urgency. When a novelist like the late Albert Camus counsels modern man to follow the "path of sympathy" and learn "how to become a saint . . . without God"; and when he declares that "Man is that force which ultimately cancels all tyrants and gods. He is the force of evidence [and] . . . must create happiness in order to protest against the universe of unhappiness," Epicurus again appears before us with prophetic grace and dignity. Similarly, when a great living writer like E. M. Forster tells us that there is "nothing that can stop your retreating into splendour and beauty—into the thoughts and beliefs that make the real life—the real you"; or when he ennobles the "generous impulses" while indicting a world crammed with "ornaments that do not adorn, features that feature nothing, flatness, meanness, uniformity without harmony, bigness without size," Epicurus' pronouncements, far from being wanting of vitality or shirking responsibility, come down through the centuries without their relevancy diminished or their wisdom impaired.

As we look back on Epicurus, it is an immanent religious quality which radiates in his teachings, that of piety, the wellspring of virtue itself. Now it is this piety which can be seen as underlying Epicurus' nonconformity and which caused him in his own time to repudiate official religion, which, with its imposition of superstitions and illusions, culminated, he contended, in the supreme sin: inhumanity. In his garden, Epicurus and his disciples carried on a nonviolent resistance to this inhumanity. Such dissenters are always the real heroes. For in their efforts they strive, to borrow Tolstoy's terms, for "a new comprehension of life" enabling man finally to move out of "the circle of violence." Their strength they draw from the deepest sources: from reason and prudence and inspiration and example.

As we look back on Epicurus, too, we can but feel pangs of regret for the unfair treatment accorded him through the centuries. Though the founder of an ennobling philosophy, he was treated as a blasphemer. Though a gentle humanist, he was viewed as a criminal. Though an ascetic, he was called a lecher. Yet it is not difficult for us to understand the reasons for this scorn. After all, Epicurus had nothing tangible to present to a state which thrives on organization and bigness. Indeed, he would rather betray his country than a friend. He sought for the calm beauty of a garden, for the affections of the heart, for the graces of character, for the relaxed will. The high decisions made in council halls; the conquests of new lands by mighty legions; the glorification of brute-masters: these for Epicurus disclosed man's continuing imprisonment in "the circle of violence."

In time Epicurus' followers found themselves alienated from the life around them, since they refused to seek after strange gods.

Their refusal to share in this search led to many reprisals and after the fourth century A.D. the Epicureans were heard of less and less. Ever following the words of Epicurus, ever believing in the joys of friendship and the blessings of peace, they could no longer escape the crushing footfalls of armies, and thus they paid the highest penalty for their dissenting faith and serene vision. Many disappeared. Others became anonymous. Still revering Epicurus, their august teacher of peace, they could do nothing more than wait and hope for better days, days which stretch stubbornly over centuries of strange silence and of ruin and desecration.

GEORGE ANDREW PANICHAS

College Park, Maryland

Acknowledgments

Dr. Charles D. Murphy, Head of the Department of English, University of Maryland, encouraged me from the beginning and in numerous ways to write this book.

Mr. N. Frederick Nash, of the University of Maryland Library, provided me with valuable bibliographical materials. He discussed with me various aspects of the book and read and discerningly criticized some of the chapters, especially the final one, which owes much to his suggestions.

Miss Martha Seabrook, of the University of Maryland Library, gave freely of her time in stylizing the manuscript, as well as in making pertinent recommendations concerning the approach of the book. I am indeed grateful to her for detecting flaws that might otherwise have remained in the book.

Miss Mary Slayton patiently typed the various drafts of the manuscript and compiled the Index. Her sensitive literary responses, her judicious criticisms, and above all her enthusiasm for the book helped at all times to stimulate both the research and the writing. Without her constant support I could not have written this volume.

The General Research Board of the University of Maryland provided generous financial assistance which enabled me to pursue the research and the writing of the book.

To the Librarians and Staffs of the Library of Congress (Washington, D. C.), of the Mt. Holyoke College Library (South Hadley, Mass.), of the Springfield (Mass.) City Library, and of the University of Maryland Library (College Park), I want to express my thanks for the assistance that they gave me.

Others who have helped me in different ways are Professor A. Owen Aldridge, Miss Betty B. Baehr, Mr. George Allan Cate, Dr. John E. George, Professor Mary P. Gianos, Professor Roderick

Jellema, Mr. John A. Koumoulides, Professor Vivian de Sola Pinto, Professor John E. Rexine, and Miss Margaret Rose.

It is almost unnecessary for me to say that any errors which appear in this book are my own.

Contents

Biology

Chronology

The school is organized as a fellowship, the main and constant goal being the moral perfection of the students through the achievement of tranquillity of mind and freedom from pain.

As head of the school, Epicurus is venerated by his adherents.

He writes three hundred books, but of his writings only the *Letters* to Herodotus, to Pythocles, and to Menoeceus, and the forty *Principal Doctrines* survive.

271 Death comes to Epicurus after a painful illness lasting a fortnight.

Epicurus' successors carry on unaltered his teachings, which attract many followers not only in Greece and in the Greco-Oriental world (*e.g.*, in Antioch, Judaea, and Egypt) but eventually also in Italy, particularly in Rome, and in Roman Africa.

✱ Epicureanism flourishes as an organized movement for seven centuries, three centuries before Christ and four afterward.

CHAPTER 1

Life

THE history of civilization bears weary witness to the abuse and the punishment inflicted periodically on nonconformist thinkers in politics, science, religion, art, and philosophy. Although essential to the improvement of the human weal, fierce independence of opinion is an indulgence which few will let themselves support. To do so requires extraordinary moral stature: "Only great men," Saint Augustine tells us, "have brought forth heresies." [1] Among those rare hardy souls braving the wrath of their contemporaries by choosing to question the conventions and beliefs of their times, there is Epicurus, the ancient Greek teacher and philosopher.

As Diogenes Laertius, a Greek biographer who lived in the early part of the third century after Christ, points out in Book X of his *Lives and Opinions of Eminent Philosophers*, Epicurus was not only misrepresented but also slandered by his enemies. He was regarded as one of the "most shameless of the physicists," a "foul-mouthed bastard," a flatterer of persons in important positions, a plagiarizer of the doctrines of Democritus about atoms and of Aristippus about pleasure, a teacher of effeminacy, a lewd letter-writer, and a nasty name-caller. His calumniators contended that he used to go around with his mother to houses and read superstitious chants of purification, that he assisted in his father's elementary school for a miserable pittance, that he vomited twice a day from overindulgence, that one of his brothers was a pimp, that his acquaintance with philosophy was small and with life even smaller, and that he wantonly counseled, "Hoist all sail, my dear boy, and steer clear of all culture." [2]

To a large degree, then, Epicurus suffered the fate of a heretic. Indeed, his fate was similar to that of other heretics who through the centuries have been reviled and portrayed as persons infected with spiritual leprosy, surrendering their souls to the devil and seducing good men to evil. Yet, it is easily forgotten that a heretic has much in common with a saint and a prophet:

He is the extreme antithesis of the indifferentist. . . . The heretic is in deadly earnest; he does not straddle the fence. He courageously accepts the consequences of his actions. His fervor can teach us the meaning of loyalty to truth. We may even say that the heretic embodies the religious spirit in concentrated form.[3]

No other words, to be sure, could better capture the meaning of and the impulses behind Epicurus' thought and mission. Diogenes Laertius, in fact, asserts unreservedly that Epicurus' critics were "stark mad" and totally ignorant of an abundance of evidence attesting to the philosopher's excellence of character. As examples of this excellence he cites Epicurus' "unsurpassed goodwill" to his country, which honored him with bronze statues; to his friends, who could be counted by whole cities; and to his intimates, who were "held fast . . . by the siren-charms of his doctrine." He goes on to note that whereas other schools of philosophy were short-lived, Epicurus' school continued without interruption for centuries. His gratitude to his parents, his generosity to his brothers, his kindness to his house slaves, his reverence for the gods, his love of country: these, Diogenes Laertius maintains, underscored Epicurus' gentleness, humanity, simplicity, and reasonableness.[4]

I *Family and Early Training*

Epicurus was the son of Neocles and Chaerestrate, who belonged to the Attic deme of Gargettus and to the distinguished family of the Philaidae. In 352 or 351 B.C. his parents were among the Athenians who settled on the island of Samos, a member of the Athenian confederacy, which experienced much political discord over the years. The settlers, called cleruchs, retained their Athenian citizenship as they accumulated colonial possessions. Epicurus was born in Samos early in February, 341 B.C., and he remained there until 323. His family included three other sons— Neocles, Chaeredemus, and Aristobulus. That their life together was harmonious and happy is indicated by Epicurus' abiding loyalty and devotion to his parents and to his brothers.

Epicurus probably received his earliest education from his father, who was a schoolmaster. Indeed, his detractors went so far as to deride him as the son of an obscure elementary school teacher (*grammatodidaskalos*). (In the ancient world this level of teaching was considered "one of the last shifts of impecuniosity.")[5] It is evident that while still a child he showed remarkable intellectual curiosity as well as independent and even rebellious attitudes. According to an account by Sextus Empiricus, Epicurus at the age of fourteen turned to philosophy in disgust because his teacher of language and literature could not explain to him the meaning of chaos in Hesiod's *Theogony*.[6] The teacher to whom he turned was the Platonist Pamphilus, under whom he apparently studied for four years. In a Platonic school he probably received thorough training in geometry, as was the custom of the times.

In 323, the year of Alexander's death, when Xenocrates was lecturing at the Academy and Theophrastus at the Lyceum, and when Aristotle, to avoid persecution by the anti-Macedonian party in Athens, retired to Chalcis, Epicurus went to Athens to begin his two-year term of military service. Menander, the future poet of the New Comedy, happened to be his fellow cadet (*ephēbos*). No doubt Epicurus' intellectual interests at this time were curtailed because of the demands of his cadetship. Presumably, however, he managed to attend some of the lectures given by Xenocrates and even some by Theophrastus.

II *Colophon*

With the completion of his military duties in 321, Epicurus rejoined his family in Colophon, in Asia Minor, one of the seven cities claiming to be the birthplace of Homer. The Athenian settlers of Samos had been forced to move to Colophon upon the order of Perdiccas, the Macedonian regent of Asia. Epicurus remained here until 311, his ten-years' stay becoming of great importance in the development of his philosophy. This was a period of "solitary reflexion and meditation," at the end of which "he emerged as a self-confident and independent thinker with a fully developed and neatly integrated body of doctrine."[7]

During the early part of the Colophon period, as the historian Apollodorus reports, Epicurus studied briefly under Praxiphanes, a famous Peripatetic teacher in Rhodes. Epicurus himself denied having studied in Rhodes. (A modern scholar, however, inclines to the belief that Epicurus did study under Praxiphanes, who in

all likelihood instructed his pupils in the skill of "good writing.")[8]
What is certain is that Epicurus studied under Nausiphanes, a
Democritean atomist who taught in the Ionian city of Teos, not
far from Colophon. Nausiphanes had been a pupil of a Skeptic
teacher, Pyrrho of Elis (*ca.* 360–270 B.C.), and was captivated by
the latter's "imperturbability," saying that "we should follow
Pyrrho in disposition but himself in doctrine." [9]

Pyrrho stressed that real things are inaccessible to human
knowledge and advised that a wise man should be indifferent
(*adiaphoros*) to "vain pursuits" and "childish folly," so that nothing may disturb his equanimity (*ataraxia*). Pyrrho was especially
fond of Democritus and of Homer. Often and approvingly he
would repeat these words from the *Iliad* (VI. 146): "As leaves on
trees, such is the life of man." He also taught that throughout life
man should suspend judgments, for he denied "that anything was
honourable or dishonourable, just or unjust. And so, universally,
he held that there is nothing really existent, but custom and convention govern human action; for no single thing is in itself any
more than that." [10]

In his biography of Pyrrho, Diogenes Laertius reports that Epicurus greatly admired Pyrrho's way of life and often asked Nausiphanes for information about him. Perhaps Epicurus' fundamental belief in the need for tranquillity can be traced to this phase of
his education. In later years, however, Epicurus denounced
Pyrrho as an "uneducated fool." But this was only one of his numerous angry attacks on other philosophers. He is said to have
called the followers of Plato "flatterers of Dionysus"; Aristotle a
"profligate"; Protagoras "a copier of Democritus"; Heraclitus a
"confusion-maker"; and the Cynics "enemies of Hellas." [11] Such invective was part of the controversy raging among the various
schools of philosophy in Athens during and after the fourth century B.C. Moreover, Epicurus' desire not to be thought influenced
by or even associated with any other philosopher was so intense
that he insisted he was "self-taught."

As a student Epicurus was persistently troublesome and defiant,
revealing traits which, as already seen, had appeared in his boyhood when he argued with his teacher over Hesiod. In truly nonconformist fashion he spoke his mind bluntly and refused to
subscribe to Nausiphanes' beliefs. So vehement were his disagree-
ments with his teacher that he condemned Nausiphanes as one

who "had the sophist's off-hand boastfulness like many another servile soul." Furthermore, in calling Nausiphanes a "fraud" and a "trollop," Epicurus was unquestionably showing his disdain for his teacher's morality. "As for my own opinion," Epicurus writes in respect to Nausiphanes, "I presume that the high-steppers [Platonists] will think me really a pupil of the 'lung-fish' and that I listened to his lectures in the company of certain lads who were stupid from the night's carousing. For he was both an immoral man and addicted to such practices as made it impossible for him to arrive at wisdom." [12]

For the most part Epicurus addressed himself to independent study and meditation during his years in Colophon. Here, undoubtedly, he shaped the main elements of his doctrine, in particular his theory of the search for the good life by means of discussion and reason. "Let no young man delay the study of philosophy," he writes in one of his letters, "and let no old man become weary of it; for it is never too early nor too late to care for the well-being of the soul." [13]

III *Mytilene and Lampsacus*

By 311 it was time for Epicurus to apply and to test his doctrine. It was time for a theorist to become a teacher. He gained his first teaching experiences in the city of Mytilene on the island of Lesbos, which had been a brilliant center of civilization in the seventh century B.C., when the poets Alcaeus and Sappho and the statesman Pittacus flourished there. In a later century Aristotle, before going to Macedon as the young Alexander's tutor, had taught on the island. And Theophrastus, who succeeded Aristotle as head of the Peripatetic School, was born on Lesbos about 372 B.C.

Epicurus stayed in Mytilene for only one year, for the opposition to his teachings, which were viewed as impious, was becoming violent. Perhaps reports of his bitter quarrel with Nausiphanes and of his dogmatism had preceded him to Mytilene. In any case Epicurus' disdain for rhetoric, dialectic, and mathematics aroused the animosity of the followers of Plato and of Aristotle. In fact, because of the controversy and the bitterness that his teachings generated in Mytilene, Epicurus was forced to escape to Lampsacus, a city in the northwest part of Asia Minor, near the Hellespont.

From 310 till 306 Epicurus remained in Lampsacus. Here, having managed to gain official promises of protection, he concentrated on attracting followers. Already, while in Mytilene, he had made a convert of Hermarchus, who was later to be his successor as head of the school in Athens. In Lampsacus he went on to earn the lifelong friendship and loyalty of Metrodorus, Idomeneus, Leonteus and his wife Themista, Colotes, Polyaneus, and Pythocles. Some of these followers, like Idomeneus, were men of distinction and means who were able to help Epicurus financially.

Even at this early date Epicurus displayed a gift for inspiring disciples and friends. He strongly believed that of all conditions providing for the happiness of man, the most important is friendship. A quintessential doctrine of Epicurean philosophy, therefore, revolves around the conception that "the same wisdom that permits us to be confident that no evil is eternal or even of long duration also recognizes that in our limited state the security that can be most perfectly gained is that of friendship." [14]

IV *Athens*

By 306 Epicurus was prepared to establish his own school in Athens. From the standpoint of steadfast supporters, financial resources, personal security, and program of instruction, he was now ready to begin his lifework, to commence his ministry, so to speak. That he chose to do so in Athens is no surprise. Described by a poet as "the eye of Greece, mother of arts, /And eloquence," [15] Athens was celebrated for its philosophers, its schools, its intellectual fervor.

In the summer of 306, during the archonship of Anaxicrates, Epicurus returned to Athens. For a while, Diogenes Laertius relates, he pursued his studies "in common with the other philosophers, but afterwards put forward independent views by the foundation of the school called after him." [16] He remained in Athens for the rest of his life, though on several occasions he did leave the city, but only for brief intervals, when he traveled to Ionia to visit friends.

Epicurus, it should be emphasized, did not offer public instruction in Athens. His school differed from the Academy and the Lyceum in that it was a private school. Interestingly enough, too, it was the first school of philosophy to admit women. The property of the school, located in a section of Athens called Melite, comprised a house and a small garden nearby, which Epicurus had purchased for eighty minae. Because he did not believe that property should be held in common, a Pythagorean practice which he felt implied mistrust among friends, Epicurus was the sole owner of the building and the garden.

Many friends and enthusiasts, both men and women, came to live with him, forming an intimate brotherhood or community of believers. "Friend," read the words inscribed on Epicurus' school, "here it will be well for you to abide; here pleasure is the highest good." Horace's slanderous reference to the "fat sleek swine of Epicurus' herd" [17] ignores the facts of Epicurean asceticism. Proof is inescapable that Epicurus and his "fellow-students" lived "a very simple and frugal life . . . content with half a pint of thin wine and were, for the rest, thoroughgoing water-drinkers." Epicurus himself set the example of a man of simple wants and of clean living. "Send me a little pot of cheese," we hear him gently saying, "that, when I like, I may fare sumptuously." [18]

The organization of Epicurus' school, as well as of later Epicurean groups, was based on a system of mutual benevolence, voluntary cooperation, and friendship. Though the teachers were distinguished by various ascending ranks and though there were organized classes and tutorial groups, the central goal of all concerned, of leaders and of followers alike, was moral purification. The students were not taught as such but rather were guided in attaining wisdom and happiness, both by emulating and by revering the way of life of the founder of the school, to whom they pledged: "We will be obedient to Epicurus, according to whom we have made it our choice to live." The correction of faults through voluntary discipline was administered not only by the head of the school but also by teachers of lower ranks, or even by students: ". . . the leaders were themselves followers, and their adherents were followers of followers. They differed from one another only in the degree of their advancement toward wisdom." Gentleness, persuasion, sympathy, compassion, and complete honesty and firmness characterized this process. Epicurean education, in short, sought to bring about the moral perfection of the individual.[19]

V *Writings and Secondary Sources*

During his remaining years, while he served as the lovable master of his school, Epicurus wrote about three hundred rolls or "books." The titles of these include *On Nature* (in thirty-seven books), *On Atoms and Void, On Love, On Choice and Avoidance, On the End, On the Gods, On Piety, On Human Life* (in four books), *On Just Dealing, On Vision, On Touch, On Fate, On Images, On Music, On Justice and Other Virtues, On Benefits and Gratitude, On Kingship,* and *On Diseases and Death.* Unfortunately, with the exception of the writings preserved by Diogenes Laertius, that is, the *Letters* to Herodotus, to Pythocles, and to Menoeceus—relating to natural philosophy, meteorology, and ethical theory respectively—and the forty *Principal Doctrines,* there are no remains of his work. Diogenes Laertius' "Life of Epicurus" (Book X), culled from many earlier works which have not survived, is generally accepted as the authority for Epicurus' life and writings. He is viewed, however, as an uncritical and unphilosophical compiler, though Montaigne wished that there had been not one Diogenes Laertius but a dozen.

There are, to be sure, some additional sources for our knowledge of his thought. In 1888 a collection variously called *The Sayings of Epicurus, The Vatican Sayings,* and *The Vatican Collection of Aphorisms* was discovered in a fourteenth-century manuscript in the Vatican Library. This collection comprises eighty-one apothegms from Epicurus' works and from his correspondence, in addition to repetitions from his *Principal Doctrines.* It also includes some quotations from the works of Metrodorus, Epicurus' beloved disciple, who died before him.

During the years 1752–54 excavations at Herculaneum, an ancient city on the gulf of Naples, produced nearly two thousand papyri. A large number of these contained the treatises of Epicureans, particularly of Philodemus, a popular teacher in Rome in the first century B.C., but only fragments of them have been decipherable. Famous for its buildings and libraries, Herculaneum was completely covered with lava in A.D. 79, following the eruption of Mt. Vesuvius. There is reason to believe that the charred papyrus fragments once constituted the library of a wealthy Roman, Calpurnius Piso, patron of Philodemus and father-in-law of Julius Caesar.

Another source of information is the stone inscriptions discovered by two French archeologists, Holleaux and Paris, in the town of Oenoanda in Lycia, Asia Minor, in 1884. These inscriptions, covering a space about forty-five yards long, were made in the second century after Christ by a certain Epicurean teacher, Diogenes, who carved his version of Epicurean doctrine on the walls of the marketplace.

The most celebrated secondary source for information about Epicurus' thought is the didactic poem *On the Nature of Things*, by the great Roman poet and passionate exponent of Epicureanism, Titus Lucretius Carus (*ca*. 99–55 B.C.). He expresses his debt to Epicurus in these words:

Thou, father, art discoverer of things, thou furnishest us with fatherly precepts, and like as bees sip of all things in the flowery lawns, we, O glorious being, in like manner feed from out thy pages upon all the golden maxims, golden I say, most worthy ever of endless life.[20]

There is helpful information, too, in the works of such later writers as Cicero, Plutarch, Aetios, Seneca, Sextus Empiricus, Joannes Stobaeus, and Athenaeus.

VI   Death and Will

Epicurus died in 271 B.C., during the archonship of Pytharatus. His health had always been delicate, and the end came after an illness which lasted just a fortnight. Diogenes Laertius informs us that Epicurus, with his customary serenity, entered a bronze bath of hot water, drank some unmixed wine, and after bidding his friends to remember his doctrine, breathed his last. Shortly before his death, he had written to Idomeneus:

On this happy day, which is also the last day of my life, I write the following words to you. The symptoms of my strangury and dysentery are continuing and have not lost their extreme seriousness. But offsetting all this is the joy in my heart at the recollection of the conversations we have had. Take charge of the children of Metrodorus, as behooves one who from boyhood on has been attached to me and to philosophy.[21]

Epicurus' will testifies to his allegiance to his friends and disciples and to his deep concern for the welfare of their children. Of his slaves he freed Mys, Nicias, Lycon, and Phaedrium, a female slave. Characteristically, he made financial provisions so that "none of those members of the school who have rendered service to me in private life and have shown me kindness in every way and have chosen to grow old with me in the school should, so far as my means go, lack the necessaries of life." [22]

Another stipulation which Epicurus made in his will, attesting at the same time to his hope that his heirs would "preserve to the best of their power the common life in the garden in whatever way is best," was the continuance of the practice of observing feast-days in honor of his parents, his brothers, and his friends, including Epicurus' birthday. He requested that the school commemorate himself and Metrodorus on the twentieth day of each month. (From the Greek word for the twentieth day, *eikas,* the Epicureans were thus called *eikadistae,* that is, twentieth-day men.) At these monthly celebrations—comparable in some ways to saints' days in the Christian calendar—the Epicurean brotherhood was to meet together to show sympathy for departed friends not by mourning them but by meditating on their lives. "We should find solace for misfortune," Epicurus says, "in the happy memory of the things that are gone and in the knowledge that what has come to be cannot be undone." [23]

CHAPTER 2

Atomism

EPICURUS' attempts to explain the nature of the physical universe, to identify the ultimate matter, the stuff, out of which the world is made, cannot be viewed as being completely revolutionary or wholly original. His theories encompass only part of a long line of development in Greek scientific thought, going back, in fact, three centuries before him to Thales (*ca.* 625–546 B.C.), who has been termed the "first man of science," the father of philosophy and astronomy, and who was revered as one of the Seven Wise Men of ancient times. Indeed, Epicurus' concepts of natural, sensible phenomena, as well as his search for an understanding of the material principle of things, were preceded not only by Thales but also by such famous "physiologists" as Anaximander, Anaximenes, Heraclitus, Parmenides, Empedocles, Anaxagoras, Leucippus, and Democritus. Hence, Epicurus must share with these other Greek heralds of enlightenment any credit for advances made against superstition and myth relating to the nature of the world.

One of the most important endeavors of ancient Greek philosophy, according to a distinguished Israeli physicist, Samuel Sambursky, in his book *The Physical World of the Greeks,* was to interpret by reason natural manifestations which had been interpreted heretofore by mythologies. "Greek science's achievement of independence," writes Sambursky, "through the struggle of logos against mythos is in many respects similar to the birth of modern science from the assault on petrified mediaeval scholasticism. With the study of nature set free from the control of mythological fancy, the way was opened for the development of science as an intellectual system." [1]

I *The Milesian School*

The beginnings of a theory of physical existence and of an independent scientific approach can be traced back to the early sixth century B.C. and, more specifically, to pre-Socratic philosophy, which marks the origins of Greek natural philosophy. Of course, because only fragments have survived of the writings of this period, we must depend on secondhand sources for our knowledge of the earliest Greek science. At any rate, it is evident that the cradle of Greek philosophy was Ionia, a region of ancient Asia Minor occupying a narrow coastal strip of what is today western Turkey and the neighboring Aegean Islands. Here Greeks had settled, supposedly before 1000 B.C. Ionic philosophy, as it no doubt deserves to be called, originated with Thales and with his two fellow Ionians and "associates," Anaximander (*ca.* 610–545 B.C.) and Anaximenes (*ca.* 585/4–528/4 B.C.). Because they were citizens of the great seaport of Miletus, these three men make up what is called the Milesian School.

Rejecting any belief in an absolute becoming and passing away, as well as postulating that there are a number of eternal and unchangeable primordial substances, or elements, these thinkers set out to speak in terms of nature. "What we discern in their background," Giorgio de Santillana rightly observes, "are not priests and prophets, but legislators, engineers, and explorers." [2] Thales, the founder of the Milesian School and the originator of Ionic natural philosophy, was the first physiologist concerned with the material unity of the cosmos. (It is of interest that Thales was teaching his theory of physical unity at the same time when the Jews, in the ministries of the great Prophets, were postulating the moral unity of the cosmos.) Though the details of Thales' reasoning are lost, he is said to have taught a doctrine of the unity of matter and life, according to which nature is endowed with life and life is inseparably connected with matter. Because he believed that one substance, which he identified as water, is the primary substance of all nature and the cause of all things, Thales has been termed a monist.

On the other hand, Anaximander, considered the oldest prose writer and the earliest philosophical author, was "the first to state some of the fundamental problems of science; his answers were too bald and premature, but not in their own background irrational." [3] The basic material substance of all things, Anaximander stated, is "infinite," "unlimited," "undefined," "eternal and ageless." This substance, indeterminate in quality and infinite in quantity, is the cause and the basis of all things, including the world, and is that into which all things will pass. To this substance Anaximander gave the name *apeiron*. Furthermore, he claimed that there is a periodic alternation of creation and destruction in the universe, leading to a succession of worlds without beginning or end. Noting the eternal, circular motion of the world process, he concluded that innumerable worlds evolve from an originally fluid state.

The third member of the Milesian school, Anaximenes, believed that the basic substance of all things is air. Infinite in its extent and perpetually moving, air causes all life and motion in living things, he theorized. Advancing beyond the work of his two predecessors, Anaximenes taught that air undergoes the constant changes of condensation (contraction) when it becomes wind and progressively clouds, water, earth, and stones, and of rarefaction (loosening) when it becomes fire. Furthermore, he pictured the earth as a table-like disc floating on air. "Just as our soul, being air, holds us together," he said, "so do breath and air encompass the whole world." [4] Obviously, as naïve and extraordinary as these views of the Milesians were, they marked, Zeller reminds us, "a powerful, fundamental change from a mythical conception to a natural, that is scientific, explanation of the world." [5]

II *Heraclitus*

When we come to Heraclitus (*ca.* 544–484 B.C.), perhaps the most profound and important of the pre-Socratic philosophers, we are able to see the continuation of Ionic monism, though a new and provocative question was now posed: In what way do the multiplicity and the variety of individual beings arise from the one primordial substance which is the basis of all things? A native of Ephesus in Asia Minor, Heraclitus was a colorful and controversial philosopher of whose work a number of significant fragments have survived. Often referred to as the "Obscure" because of his cryptic style, he was labeled a "muddler" by Epicurus. Earlier, Socrates had even claimed that "a champion diver" was needed to reach his meaning. Aristocratic, scornful, melancholy, Heraclitus detested the masses, believing that men "hold aloof from truth and justice." So critical of men's "wicked folly" was he that, according to Diogenes Laertius, "he would retire to the temple of Artemis and play at knuckle-bones with the boys; and when the Ephesians stood round him and looked on, 'Why, you rascals,' he said, 'are you astonished? Is it not better to do this than to take part in your civil life?' " [6] Nor is it insignificant that he believed that "war is the father of all and the king of all." [7]

In characterizing the universe as undergoing constant, harmonious, balanced change, with all things passing away and nothing abiding (*panta rei*), Heraclitus hypothesized that ethereal fire comprises the primary and eternal substance of all things, all matter, in short, of the world. (We can understand why the Stoics venerated a philosopher who anticipated their belief in the "divine spark of fire.") Or, as he firmly declares in one fragment: "This world, which is the same for all, no one of gods or men has made; but it was ever, is now, and ever shall be an ever-living Fire, with measures of it kindling, and measures going out." [8] Fire, he contended, burns without interruption, always consuming fuel, always liberating smoke. Consequently, all things are transformed into fire and then from fire into all other things, as a double process incessantly goes on, causing the materialization of fire-spirit, so to speak, and the re-spiritualization of earth and water. Diogenes Laertius sums up this process in the following way:

. . . all that is is limited and forms one world. And it is alternately born from fire and again resolved into fire in fixed cycles to all eternity, and this is determined by destiny. Of the opposites that which tends to birth or creation is called war and strife, and that which tends to destruction by fire is called concord and peace. [9]

Diogenes Laertius here underlines Heraclitus' belief that the whole of reality is like an ever-flowing stream: Nothing is ever at rest for a moment; the substance of things is always in flux. All things are in a process of transition, constant change comprising the wonder of the world. "We step and do not step into the same rivers," Heraclitus asserts; "we are and are not." "You cannot step twice into the same rivers," he further notes; "for fresh waters are ever flowing in upon you." Amid this flux the real weariness is continuance in the same state, and the real rest is change. The upward path is nothing without the downward path; and if either were to cease, the other, too, would cease and the world would disappear, for it takes both to make an apparently stable reality. All things, Heraclitus thus indicates, were produced in opposition.

Wisdom itself is actually the perception of the underlying unity of warring opposites: "Men do not know how what is at variance agrees with itself. It is an attunement of opposite tensions, like that of the bow and the lyre." Cessation of strife in the world would mean its destruction, just as the disappearance of hunger, disease, and weariness would mean the disappearance of satisfaction, health, and rest. Similarly, men would not have known the name of justice, were there no injustice: "God is day and night, winter and summer, war and peace, surfeit and hunger." [10]

III *Parmenides*

Known as the grandfather of rationalism and "the father of materialism," Parmenides (*ca.* 540–470 B.C.) was the last of the philosophers who sought to explain the world in terms of a single ultimate reality. He lived in Elea in southern Italy, where he took an active part in politics. With the exception of Empedocles (*ca.* 495–435 B.C.), Parmenides was the only Greek who wrote philosophy in verse. Unlike the monists before him, who had started with the evidence of the senses, he taught that the knowledge of reality begins with reason and not sense perception. "But do thou restrain thy thought from this way of inquiry," reads one of his fragments, "nor let habit by its much experience force thee to cast upon this way a wandering eye or sounding ear or tongue; but judge by argument the much disputed proof uttered by me." [11] Thought, or visualization, he stressed, is the touchstone of existence, for what is, is, and what is not, is not, because it cannot be thought.

Being cannot have a beginning or a ceasing to be, for it cannot be created from Non-Being or reduced to Non-Being. It was never and never will be, but is *now*, continuous and undivided. That which exists, Being, is solid, undifferentiated, motionless—an unchanging sphere, uncreated and indestructible, with nothing, not even empty space, around it. Since there is no absolute "becoming or passing away," no birth, no death, only the existent is thinkable, and only the thinkable is real. In this respect, Parmenides was the first to declare that the world is a spherical, motionless, corporeal plenum, with no such thing as empty space inside or outside. For Parmenides, then, the primary substance became a "thing in itself," a Parmenidean "Being." The early Ionians believed that all things are one; but Parmenides showed that, if this one thing really *is*, then we must give up the idea that it can take different forms.

IV *Empedocles*

It is to the fifth-century Greek philosopher Empedocles that "we owe a vital theoretical addition to the foundations of science: the concept of the dependence of phenomena on universal forces at work in the cosmos." He was the first to distinguish matter from force and "to postulate the reality of causes in the physical world and to identify them with forces." [12] In forming a new concept of matter and, above all, in abandoning the monistic hypothesis, Empedocles nevertheless agreed with Parmenides that the world is spherical and eternal, without beginning or end, without empty space. A citizen of Acragas (Agrigentum), a Greek colony on the southern coast of Italy, he was a man of prodigious accomplishment. Admired as a politician, a seer, a poet, a social reformer, and a physicist, he was also revered as a religious teacher and a physician and diviner.

Empedocles is known as a pluralist because he said that the sphere is composed of four "primary" substances, the "four roots" of all things (*tessara tōn pantōn*), which he identified as earth, air, fire, and water. Each, he asserted, is eternal, uncreated, indestructible, unchanging. To these four substances he joined two moving, corporeal, and active forces causing cosmic occurrences and comprising continuously alternating motions of attraction and repulsion: "dread Strife . . . of equal weight to each [of the elements], and Love . . . equal in length and breadth." [13] Love, a harmonious, centripetal force, brought about "the union of unlikes" and the separation of like things, whereas Strife, a discordant, centrifugal force, brought about the union of like to like and the separation of unlike things.

V *Anaxagoras*

Another important pluralist, Anaxagoras of Clyzomenae in Asia Minor (500–428 B.C.), was, Zeller insists, "consciously and deliberately the first pure contemplative thinker, who saw in knowledge of the world the task and end of life and was fully convinced of its incidental ethical effects." The first philosopher to settle in Athens, he lived there from 480–450 B.C., when he was banished on charges of impiety. As a pluralist Anaxagoras taught that primary existence contains an unlimited number of "seeds" (*spermata*) which are infinitely different. Matter, he believed, cannot be created or destroyed, for it is eternal and infinitely divisible. A thing, he continues, can be formed only of that which is like itself; each thing contains portions of all things, or as Anaxagoras states: "In everything there is a portion of everything. . . ." [14] Each thing, finally, is that of which it contains the most.

His major contribution was his belief that Mind (Nous), which differs from matter, is a moving force shaping the world. Originally, he felt, there existed an orderless mixture of "seeds," but Mind, the finest among all things (*leptotaton pantōn chrēmatōn*), simple, unmixed, passionless, "alone by itself," wherever present in matter, caused a movement of extreme swiftness taking the form of rotation, first of all of a small portion of matter, and then of more and more in an ever-increasing whirl. Anaxagoras' concept of Mind is more or less on the same level as Empedocles' concept of Love and Strife, in so far as it was instrumental in the separating of the mixed mass when "all things are together." It is no exaggeration, then, that Burnet, in his estimation of the concept of Nous, credits Anaxagoras with introducing a spiritual note into philosophy [15] (despite the fact that both Plato and Aristotle complained that he failed to express his new principle in teleological terms).

VI   *The Atomist Theory*

Atomism embodies the final development of pluralism. Leucippus, Democritus, and Epicurus were the great champions of the atomist theory, which in the ancient world was often equated with iconoclasm, impiety, and atheism, in so far as the atomists conceived of the world as resulting from chance motions and random collisions of material particles. In its broadest sense, atomism means the reduction of complex phenomena to fixed unit factors. It is a theory based on the law of the permanence of matter and on the belief that there is an infinity of separate particles, or atoms, scattered in the infinity of empty space. The atomist theory "showed that the plurality and flux of the macrocosm," to quote again from Sambursky, "can be explained by a certain uniformity and by causal laws governing the world not accessible to our senses." [16] It is interesting to note that in seeking to reconcile, or synthesize, the unity of the cosmos and the plurality of its phenomena, the atomists based their beliefs on hypotheses, on pure speculation, and not on experimentation, as employed by scientists many centuries later. In their speculations, the impelling purpose of which Democritus sums up with the words, "[I would] rather discover one cause than gain the kingdom of Persia," the atomists insisted that truth is to be found not in some other world but in the world of phenomena.[17]

VII *Leucippus*

According to Aristotle and to Theophrastus, Leucippus (fl. *ca.* 430 B.C.) can be regarded as the founder of atomism. Often his name is coupled with that of his intimate companion and disciple, Democritus (? 460–357 B.C.), who systematized, extended, and passed on his teacher's ideas. Of Leucippus' life and work not much is known. He is believed to have been a native of Abdera in Thrace, though Miletus and Elea are also cited as his place of birth. Indeed, it is not known whether he wrote anything himself, even though he is credited with writing *The Greater World System,* the basic work of atomism, and *On Mind,* of which the contents are unknown. Epicurus declined to discuss Leucippus, even claiming that no such philosopher ever existed. But, as Burnet remarks, "That would be just like Epicurus"! [18] In any case, it generally can be assumed that Leucippus was the first to establish atoms as first principles and that Democritus faithfully continued his master's work, to the point where "they stand to one another rather as the pioneer and the enthusiastic and energetic follower." [19]

Unlike Empedocles and Anaxagoras, Leucippus did not find it necessary to assume that forces like Love and Strife or a force like Mind caused motion and thus broke up original matter. For Leucippus, the atoms were of countless shapes and sizes and had been in motion for all time. As the first to affirm the existence of empty space, that is, of the void, he felt that the sum of things, the All, is unlimited. Of the All, part is full and part empty. By full, or Being, Leucippus meant matter or atoms; and by empty, or Non-Being, he meant space. Out of atoms and space arise worlds without number, which in turn dissolve into them. In a given section of the All many atoms, which are so small that they cannot be divided and which are innumerable, ever moving, and solid or "compact," are carried off into the vast empty space and are "entangled" with one another. This original motion of the atoms, taking place in all directions, causes the formation of worlds.

Diogenes Laertius describes the movement of the atoms as follows: "These collect together and form a single vortex, in which they jostle against each other and, circling round in every possible way, separate off, by like atoms joining like." Because the atoms are numerous, they cannot revolve in equilibrium. Consequently, "the light [atoms] pass into the empty space outside, as if they were being winnowed." The remaining atoms keep together and, "becoming entangled, go on their circuit together, and form a primary spherical system." [20] Leucippus further speculates that as a world is born, so, too, it grows, decays, and perishes. But nothing, he insists, "happens at random; everything happens out of reason and by necessity." [21]

VIII *Democritus*

Leucippus' atomist theory could not have survived without the efforts of Democritus of Abdera. Called the "prince of philosophers," the "laughing philosopher," and "the philosopher [who] is like the all-round athlete," Democritus was a mysterious and wonderful man, as worthy a disciple as any great master would wish to have. In his youth he was said to have been a pupil of certain Magians and Chaldeans, from whom he learned theology and astronomy. He was said to have traveled to Egypt, to Persia, to Ethiopia, even to India, where he consorted with the "naked philosophers" ("gymno-sophists"). Aloof, unassuming, solitary, contemplative, but above all precocious, he was versed in all aspects of philosophy—in physics, in ethics, in mathematics, in the arts. ("His industry . . . was so great that he cut off a little room in the garden round the house and shut himself up there.") Eventually, he was looked on as a prophet and sage by his fellow citizens, who honored him with gifts and with commemorative statues. His "universal mind" was to be reflected in his voluminous writings, of which only fragments, including some ethical aphorisms, have survived. It is said that Plato once wanted to collect and burn all the writings of Democritus but decided against the task when he realized that "there was no advantage in doing so, for already the books were widely circulated." [22]

In essence Democritus' atomist ideas are hardly distinguishable from those of Leucippus, except that they supply more details. Accepting Leucippus' beliefs that the first principles of the universe are atoms and empty space and that nothing can come into being from that which is not nor pass into that which is not, Democritus goes on to pay special attention to the atoms. Unlimited in size and number, imperceivably small and unalterable, atoms are of intrinsically different sizes and shapes and arrangements. All worlds, of which an infinite number come into being and perish, are formed of atoms and space. These worlds differ from one another in size and in other ways because the numbers, sizes, and shapes of the atoms composing them are not and can never be the same. The cause of atoms is not to be sought, for they are eternal and uncaused. Endowed with eternal motion, so that anything like divine creation or providential will is set aside, atoms are borne along in the universe in a vortex; thereby they generate all composite things such as fire, water, air, and earth, which are but conglomerations of atoms. All things happen by virtue of necessity, the vortex being the cause of the creation of all things.

Of particular importance is Democritus' theory of the ceaseless changes of reality, which he attributed to the continual aggregation or disaggregation of atoms. In this respect he theorized that some groups of atoms are subtler than others: they range from the heaviest aggregates to the lightest. These aggregates, which cause the creation of worlds, differ in the number of atoms contained and in the closeness or the laxness of their union. The size, shape, and density of a new compound are determined by these differences. Aggregates with closely compact atoms and with little void are hard and heavy; aggregates with few atoms and much void are soft and light. In the course of their movements in all directions, atoms jostle and collide with one another and become entangled in temporary combinations or aggregates. Simplicius gives the reasons for the union of atoms in compounds in this memorable passage:

. . . they [the atoms] fit into and grasp one another . . . : for some of them have uneven sides . . . , and some are hooked, some are concave, and some convex and others with innumerable varieties of shape. . . . they retain hold of one another and remain in combination until some stronger necessity from what surrounds them comes and shakes them and scatters them apart.[23]

Each aggregate falls into the particular motion of a "whirl," ultimately evolving into a world. Within even a transient combination, each atom retains its separate nature and is kept apart from other atoms by a large or a small interval of void.

It needs to be emphasized that the creation of a world, as conceived by Democritus, is the result not of chance but of inevitable natural processes that are mechanistic and deterministic. In this connection Democritus insisted that our "real" or "legitimate" knowledge is of the atoms and the void and that, above all, there is a truth beyond the senses, to be discovered through rational processes. An extant fragment from an important work of Democritus, *The Canon,* underscores his view concerning two sorts of knowledge,

. . . one genuine, one bastard. . . . To the latter belong all the following: sight, hearing, smell, taste, touch. The real is separated from this. When the bastard can do no more—neither see more minutely, nor hear, nor smell, nor taste, nor perceive by touch—and a finer investigation is needed, then the genuine comes in as having a tool for distinguishing more finely.[24]

It would be both inaccurate and unfair to Democritus, however, to think of him as only a scientist, oblivious of the demands of day-to-day living and of personal relationships. For it is clear from his extant writings, particularly from the sayings (*gnomae*) given in a collection, *Maxims of Democritus,* that his scientific preoccupations did not lead him to slight an examination of the meaning of human conduct or to evade the question "What constitutes the good life?" In Democritus a scientific outlook was combined with a deeply felt humanitarianism. His moral and ethical precepts, which rather amazingly anticipate those of Epicurus, abound with both good sense and good temper and reveal him as a humanist who was humble before the awesome fact that "we know nothing in reality; for truth lies in an abyss." [25]

Surely it is not difficult to understand why Democritus was nicknamed "Wisdom." His words are not those of a cold and austere scientist but rather those of one who yearns to improve life through the fusion of science and philosophy. The end of all human action, he declares, is tranquillity, "cheerfulness or well-being," the title, incidentally, of one of his books. His sayings further show the epigrammatic acuteness of his clear and elevated style: "Magnanimity consists in enduring tactlessness. . . ." "Neither skill nor wisdom is attainable unless one learns." "It is shameful to be so busy over the affairs of others that one knows nothing of one's own." "An enemy is not he who injures, but he who wishes to do so." "Speech is the shadow of action." "Do not try to understand everything, lest you become ignorant of everything." "One should emulate the deeds and actions of virtue, not the words." 26

Always Democritus counsels right-thinking and right-acting, for "the man who acts rightly through understanding and knowledge becomes at the same time brave and upright." The good life is attained through orderliness, good taste, and intelligence. Indeed, ". . . Chance rarely conflicts with Intelligence, and most things in life can be set in order by an intelligent sharpsightedness." The good life, furthermore, is characterized by modesty, for it "is better to be praised by another than by oneself"; by cheerfulness, which "is created for men through moderation of enjoyment and harmoniousness of life"; by inspiration, arising from "the great pleasures . . . from the contemplation of noble works"; by recreation, for the "life without festival is a long road without an inn"; and by friendship, because life "is not worth living for the man who has not even one good friend." 27

The fortunate man is he who has learned to guard against "immoderate desire" and who achieves "due measure" in his life: "The good things of youth are strength and beauty, but the flower of age is moderation." "He is fortunate," Democritus avers, "who is happy with moderate means, unfortunate who is unhappy with great possessions." The brave man, he further notes, "is not only he who overcomes the enemy, but he who is stronger than pleasures. Some men are masters of cities, but are enslaved to women." 28

Occasionally, however, Democritus reveals a touch of cynicism. His attitude toward women—"A woman is far sharper than a man in malign thoughts"—is one example of this cynicism. Another is his attitude toward children: "I do not think that one should have children. I observe in the acquisition of children many great risks and many griefs, whereas a harvest is rare, and even when it exists, it is thin and poor." 29

Yet, if there are occasional doubts in Democritus' outlook, these are far outweighed by his reverence and compassion for human life and by his intense affirmation of the tranquillity of soul which continues calm and strong, undisturbed by fears, superstitions, or "false tales about the period after the end of life." Truly Democritus was not only a scientist but also an indefatigable pilgrim seeking for the good life. Contemplating the mystery of the universe, Democritus did not fail to realize that the goal of the wise man is to bestow on others the marvelous and redeeming secrets of the good life which help one to attain the serenity that expels "those not-negligible curses in life, envy, jealousy and spite." [30]

IX   *Epicurus: A "Canonical Successor"*

It was left to Epicurus, who comes at the end of the "canonical succession" of Greek atomists, to clarify and modify Democritus' theory. Although he called the Abderite a "nonsense-monger," there can be no doubt that Epicurus drew upon him a great deal. Even though Epicurus refused to acknowledge any other philosophers in his writings, it is obvious that he made use of their ideas. Certainly, in important works like *On Nature* and *On Atoms and Void,* Epicurus must have relied extensively on his knowledge of Democritus' basic teachings on atomism. Since, unfortunately, these volumes are lost, we must concentrate on large sections of the first two books of Lucretius' poem as well as on Epicurus' *Letter to Herodotus* if we are to put together his concept of the atoms as the basis of all being.

The evidence incontestably bears witness to Cicero's claim that Democritus was "the fountain-head from which Epicurus derived the streams that watered his little garden." [31] Doubtless, there are differences between their theories, especially, for example, in that Epicurus, unlike Democritus, appeals finally to phenomena and to the realities of sense experience as proofs of his theories. It will be seen, nonetheless, that not only the inspiration but also the dominant elements of Epicurus' atomism are found in Democritus. Epicurus' theories could almost be said to contain all or most of Democritus' theories, but without the footnotes.

X   *Body and Space*

Echoes of Democritus (and even at times of Parmenides, Empedocles, and Anaxagoras) are heard in Epicurus' principles relating to a universe eternal and immutable. Nothing can be created from nothing by divine will. Nothing is resolved into nothing, for since the world was not created, it follows that it must have endured an infinite time. There are two natures: infinite matter, or body, recognized by the senses, and infinite void, or space, in which matter moves. "If what we call 'the void' or 'space' or 'impalpable being' were nonexistent, bodies would not have anywhere to exist nor would they have a medium through which to move, as they manifestly do." Matter, which is uncreated and indestructible, contains an infinite number of minute atoms, indivisible and unchangeable, "as is necessary if all is not to be dissolved to nothing." [32]

The universe, the totality of things, has always been and will always remain the same "because there is nothing into which it can change, in as much as there is nothing outside the totality that could intrude and effect change." [33] Lucretius, too, speaks of the universe as enduring for an infinite time and as remaining the same as it ever changes. He declares that "the sum of things is ever renewed and mortals live by a reciprocal dependency. Some nations wax, others wane, and in a brief space the races of living things are changed and like runners hand over the lamp of life." [34]

XI *The Atoms*

With Democritus, Epicurus concurred that the eternal atoms are the basic and imperishable constituents (seeds) of all things. They account for the persistence of all species, for "nature dissolves every thing back into its first bodies and does not annihilate things." [35] He also agreed with Democritus that the qualitative world of sense perception arises out of the ceaseless motions of qualitatively neutral atoms and that great qualitative variety arises out of the "jostlings," the collisions, of atomic aggregations. Epicurus likewise emphasized that matter is not infinitely divisible for, if it were, it would be reduced to a point of annihilation. Hence we must "exclude infinite division into smaller and smaller parts lest we make everything weak, and in our conception of the parts that compose a whole be compelled to make them less and less, finally reducing real things to nothingness." [36]

All bodies can be divided into separate parts until the stage when the lower limit of divisibility is reached, that is, when an entity is arrived at: the irreducible atom, the "invisible thing," that which, in its Greek etymological sense, cannot be divided, "cannot be cut." Wallace's admirable description of the atom is helpful at this point: "The atom is an intellectual, not a mathematical point. It has magnitude: it is not mere position. But we cannot break it up really into smaller portions. . . . It is an utmost limit of disintegration, a sort of absolute diamond, so hard that it is impossible ever to find any cleavage in it. Solidity, impenetrability, invincible resistance to any pressure, impact, or incision, seem to be the essential and primary character of the atom." [37]

Epicurus ascribed three properties to an atom: size, shape, and weight. By properties he meant essential attributes which cannot be removed or lost without the loss of a thing's identity, or as Lucretius says: "That is a property which can in no case be disjoined and separated without utter destruction accompanying the severance, such as the weight of a stone, the heat of fire, the fluidity of water." [38] The size of an atom, Epicurus believed, is neither very great nor infinitely small; rather it is extremely minute but with a lower as well as an upper limit. Allowing for variations in the sizes of atoms, he nevertheless insisted that they are not of every size, for "if they were of every size, some would necessarily be large enough for us to see." [39]

Unlike Leucippus and Democritus, who held that the number of shapes of atoms is infinite, Epicurus maintained that "the number of atoms of each shape is infinite; but the number of varieties cannot be infinite, only inconceivably great." [40] Believing that atoms have weight, Epicurus stressed that since atoms are absolutely solid with no admixture of void, their weight varies directly with their size and is the cause of their natural "downward" fall. This difference of weight, however, has no effect so far as rate of motion is concerned, for in empty space the velocity for all moving atoms is uniform.

XII *Atomic "Swerve"*

The most striking difference between the atomism of Democritus and that of Epicurus lies in the latter's theory of the atomic "swerve." Epicurus' concept of this swerve, it should be noted, is not mentioned in his *Letter to Herodotus,* the section discussing it having been lost. As happened with so much of his thought, Epicurus' "swerve of the atoms" was passed on by Lucretius, who called it the *clinamen atomorum.*[41] (Accounts are also preserved in Cicero and in Diogenes of Oenoanda.) In any event, Epicurus was not satisfied with Democritus' belief that because the "jostling" of atomic compounds is an eternal process, there is no need to bother with the origin of atomic collisions. Although a materialist, Epicurus did not believe, as did Democritus, a determinist, that atoms are always controlled by natural laws.

The atoms, Epicurus speculated, continually fall through space, not toward the center of the earth but "downwards." At the same time he was careful to point out that "we cannot predicate up or down of infinite space as if there were a highest or a lowest." Hence "up" and "down" are relative terms which have meaning only in reference to ourselves: "it is possible [he continues] to think of one motion extending to infinity in the direction that we call up and one extending down, even if what moves from us into the spaces above our heads comes a thousand times to the feet of those above us and what moves downward comes to the heads of those below. . . ." [42]

According to Epicurus' theory, atoms in the course of their downward fall accidentally collide. These atoms, despite differences of weight, continue to fall at the same velocity but no longer straight down. Rather, by an uncaused deflection from their vertical motion, that is, a swerve, atoms collide with other falling atoms, so that a complex of motions is set up. Without the swerve, Lucretius reminds us, the atoms "would all fall down, like drops of rain, through the deep void, and no clashing would have begotten nor blow produced among the first-beginnings: thus nature never would have produced aught." [43] But as the direction of the atoms is altered and a ferment of atoms arises as they move in every direction, ultimately there occurs a fortuitous union in compounds which occasions the world of sensible things.

Atomic compounds are in ceaseless movement precisely because "the motion of the whole body is the aggregate motion of its component atoms." [44] Moreover, atomic speed is not diminished as an atom moves into its compound body. In the compound the atoms are similar to free atoms in space, which are incessantly in motion, for "no rest is given to first bodies throughout the unfathomable void, but driven on rather in ceaseless and varied motion they partly, after they have pressed together, rebound leaving great spaces between, while in part they are so dashed away after the stroke as to leave but small spaces between." [45]

Lucretius notes that although "the first-beginnings of things are all in motion, yet the sum is seen to rest in supreme repose." He goes on, "all the nature of first things lies far away from our sense beneath their ken." And, because these "first things" are beyond what one can see, so too must their motions be invisible. This invisibility, he emphasizes, must not lead us to reject the internal movement in an atomic compound. Its movement is merely hidden, just as it is, for instance, in the inner movement of a mass of things seen from a great distance. In the following passage, Lucretius illustrates this premise with two analogies, a distant flock of sheep and a distant army:

Thus often the wooly flocks as they crop the glad pastures on a hill, creep on whither the grass jewelled with fresh dew summons and invites each, and the lambs fed to the full gambol and playfully butt; all which objects appear to us from a distance to be blended together and to rest like a white spot on a green hill. Again when mighty legions fill with their movements all parts of the plains waging the mimicry of war, the glitter then lifts itself up to the sky and the whole earth round gleams with brass and beneath a noise is raised by the mighty trampling of men and the mountains stricken by the shouting reecho the voices to the stars of heaven, and horsemen fly about and suddenly wheeling scour across the middle of the plains, shaking them with the vehemence of their charge. And yet there is some spot on the high hills, seen from which they appear to stand still and to rest on the plains as a bright spot.[46]

Generally commentators, ancient and modern, criticize Epicurus' swerve as an infamous contradiction of natural laws, terming it a "causeless interruption" of the principle that "nothing is created out of nothing," a violation of cause and effect: "for it is the assertion of a force for which no cause can be given and no explanation offered." [47] Attacking Epicurus' theory of the atomic swerve as "a piece of childish fancy" and "an arbitrary fiction," Cicero argues: "For, if all the atoms swerve, none will ever come to cohere together; or if some swerve while others travel in a straight line, by their own natural tendency, in the first place this will be tantamount to assigning to the atoms their different spheres of action, some to travel straight and some sideways; while secondly . . . this riotous hurly-burly of atoms could not possibly result in the ordered beauty of the world we know." [48]

Until the present day Epicurus' theory of the swerve continues to be scorned as "a complete failure and a blot on ancient materialism. It is scientific nonsense and ethical folly, and is destructive of the very values that Epicurus sought to protect." [49] But if Epicurus violated certain scientific axioms, he did so because, as Bertrand Russell suggests, he had no interest in science per se, valuing it only in so far as it provided those naturalistic explanations of phenomena that counter magic, astrology, divination, and superstition—the great enemies of the tranquil life.[50] In fact, there is some justification in Bailey's feeling that "Epicurus' [atomic] kinetics are indeed as profound an attempt to think below the surface of phenomena as any in the ancient world—even in Aristotle." [51]

Furthermore, Epicurus' theory of the atomic swerve must be examined in the light of his desire to help man escape from the blind necessity of mechanism. On the one hand, he adopted a mechanistic system so that he might repudiate fears and superstitions relating to man's organic functions and to the universe. On the other hand, he introduced into that system an unmechanistic element, the swerve, with its power of self-determination, so that he might combat the idea that destiny controls man's actions. Epicurus obviously felt that Democritus' determinism ruled out free will and made man a victim of matter.

The concept of freedom played a major role in Epicurus' ethical thinking. For the origin of freedom he went back to the atoms, specifically to the characteristics and effects of their lateral swerve. Rejecting any correlation of atomic motion with the idea of finality, he attributed to the atoms and to their movements that element of freedom which presupposes and is brought to consciousness in the human will. Thus Epicurus scorned the idea of an inexorable fate, which the mythologers and even some of the physicists had perpetuated, contending that fatalism paralyzes man's efforts to control experience and attain spiritual quietude. Epicurus thereby sought to teach that man is capable of improving himself, is capable of breaking through "the decrees of fate." "Do you," Lucretius asks, "see then in this case that, though an outward force often pushes men on and compels them frequently to advance against their will and to be hurried headlong on, there yet is something in our breast sufficient to struggle against and resist it?" [52]

This "something" it is, then, that embodies the spontaneity and the change empowering man to wrestle with and to quell the forces of circumstance and of fortune. Lacking this element, one can become, in Epicurus' phrase, like "the young man [who] at the height of his powers is unstable and is carried this way and that by fortune, like a headlong stream." [53] The human will, consequently, is analogous to the atom with its incalculable and unpredictable power to change direction, for, as Lucretius declares,

. . . in seeds too you must . . . admit that besides blows and weights there is another cause of motions, from which this power of free action has been begotten in us, since we see that nothing can come from nothing. For weight forbids that all things be done by blows through . . . an outward force; but that the mind itself does not feel an internal necessity in all its actions and is not . . . overmastered and compelled to bear and put up with this, is caused by a minute swerving of first beginnings at no fixed part of space and no fixed time.[54]

XIII   The Canon: *Sensations*

The Canon is the title that Epicurus gave to a volume, now lost, containing an introduction to his philosophical thought. He separated philosophy into three parts, Canon, Physics, and Ethics, in so far as he believed that the Ethics were deduced from the Physics and that the truth of both was subject to the test of the axiomatic part, the Canon. In the latter he sought to teach the norms of cognition and the three means of testing and of knowing truth, the three criteria: sensations, preconceptions or anticipations, and feelings. By emphasizing that the life of the senses constitutes the sole reality, Epicurus was no doubt replying particularly to Pyrrho of Elis and to his followers, known as the Skeptics, who questioned the evidence of the senses and established a philosophy "taking the form of agnosticism and suspension of judgement." [55]

Sensations, Epicurus insisted in *The Canon*, are irrefutable: "one sensation cannot convict another and kindred sensation, for they are equally valid." And reason itself cannot refute sensations "for reason is wholly dependent on sensation." Thus, too, although atoms and the void are ultimate but imperceptible realities, "it is from plain facts [our sensory experience of compound bodies] that we must start when we draw inferences about the unknown." [56] "The fact of sensation itself," stresses Epicurus, "universally attests that there are bodies, and it is by reference to sensation that we must rationally infer the existence of imperceptible bodies. . . ." [57] When errors relating to the truth of the senses arise, it is because of the addition of "opinions" or judgements":

If you reject any single sensation and fail to distinguish between the conclusion of opinion as to the appearance awaiting confirmation and that which is actually given by the sensation or feeling, or each intuitive apprehension of the mind, you will confound all other sensations as well with the same groundless opinion, so that you will reject every standard of judgement.[58]

XIV *Atomic Films*

How, then, are things perceived by the senses? This question was of much importance to Epicurus, who felt that the process of sensation was incomplete without the proof of cognition. Hence, Epicurus asserted that the surfaces of bodies continuously give off streams of particles, variously referred to as images, effluxes, outlines, filaments, husks, effluences, or atomic films (*eidola*). As these particles swiftly and unceasingly stream off existing bodies, others take their places, so that the bodies never diminish. (Here, too, Epicurus was indebted to Democritus' belief that the emission of successive films is due to the motion of the atoms which make up every concrete body.)

Sense perception is the result of atomic films impinging on the various sense organs. When we see, for instance, it is because thin films ("idols") from sensible objects pass through the intervening air and fall into our eyes to produce in us "clear images" of things and affect our minds. "Now we must suppose," Epicurus states, ". . . that it is when something enters us from external objects that we not only see but think of their shapes." [59] At this point it is perhaps worth noting that Epicurus did not agree at all with Democritus' belief that "all objects constantly give off material images of themselves, which are impressed on the air between the object and the eye, as on wax. This impression is then reflected back to the eye, into which it enters, and is communicated to the rest of the body." [60]

Concerning the texture of atomic films, Epicurus declares that "nothing among perceptible things contradicts the belief that the images have unsurpassable fineness of texture." [61] Lucretius goes on to specify that the existence of these images can even be confirmed by parallels in the visible world, and he offers the examples of "smoke which logs of oak, heat which fires emit," of "gossamer coats which at times cicades doff in summer," of the "vesture which the slippery serpent puts off among the thorns." [62] According to Epicurus, too, "the creation of the idols takes place as quick as thought," and "nothing or very few things hinder their emission by collisions." [63]

Colors, sounds, and tastes, Epicurus taught, are not qualities of the primary body but are formed only when the tiny particles from the real bodies come into contact with the organs of sense. A vivid example of this contact comes out in Epicurus' discussion of "effluences" and their relation to hearing. Hearing results "when a kind of stream is carried to our ears from a person who speaks or from an object that makes a sound or noise." The current is then split into particles, "each of which is of the same nature as the whole, and these particles preserve a common relationship to each other and a peculiar continuity that extends back to the source of the sound." "We must not suppose," he adds, "that the air itself receives an impression from the spoken word or sound, for indeed the air is far from admitting any such thing." Rather, he maintains stoutly, "the force that is created in us when we speak causes such a displacement of particles, capable of forming a breathlike stream, that it produces in the person to whom we are speaking the sensation of hearing." [64]

XV *Preconceptions and Feelings*

A second criterion of reality, according to Epicurus, preconceptions are the products of observation as well as the results of sensations. They are common to all men and afford a basis of judgment. Diogenes Laertius defines a preconception (*prolēpsis*) as an "apprehension or a right opinion or notion, or universal idea stored in the mind; that is, a recollection of an external object often presented." [65] The result of repeated aggregate sensations, a preconception is preserved in the remembrance of numerous similar perceptions of the same object. This memory-picture emerges in consciousness when words are employed to designate their respective objects, and it takes on the character of the universal, a general "opinion" which has developed out of the contact of man with things.

The most tangible result of this process is that "we are not left with a series of detached unmeaning sensations, but are enabled to correlate them, to identify and distinguish." [66] Every word, or term, that is used, therefore, must call up a "plain and clear" picture or an idea that in turn is based on a "plain and clear" perception of a recurring or accumulated form or image. In this way, Epicurus allowed for the exercise of reason in the acquisition of knowledge, though, as is to be expected, it is always subordinated to the senses, indeed derived from and ratified by them. "For the similarity between the things which exist," Epicurus explains, "which we call real, and the images received as a likeness of things and produced either in sleep or through some other acts of apprehension on the part of the mind or the other instruments of judgement, could never be, unless there were some effluences of this nature actually brought into contact with our senses." [67]

Diogenes Laertius illustrates Epicurus' theory of preconception with the word "man" which we utter when we think of a human shape, a picture of which has been given already to the mind by recollections. If the object in front of us is a horse or a cow, we must have known of the animal's shape, not by some innate idea but by a process of preconception, for "the object of a judgement is derived from something previously clear." But ultimately, it needs emphasizing, interpretation itself—"judgement," "opinion" —is true only "if it is subsequently confirmed or if it is not contradicted by evidence, and false if it is not subsequently confirmed or is contradicted by evidence." [68]

It is man's inference about sensation that leads to error. From far off, for example, a man may see the square towers of a town, but "they often appear to be round . . . [because] all the angles are seen from a distance to look obtuse, or rather are not seen at all, and their blow is lost and their stroke never makes its way to our sight, because while the idols are borne on through much air, the air by repeated collisions blunts the stroke perforce." [69] It is only when a man tests an opinion, in this case by getting close to a tower and learning that it is really square, that he can recognize the truth of the senses.

Feelings comprise the third and moral criterion of truth. There are two states of feelings, we are told, pleasure and pain, and these "arise in every animate being . . . the one is favourable and the other hostile to that being, and by their means choice and avoidance are determined." [70] Feelings, consequently, tell us whether a thing is good or bad, and as DeWitt observes, operate on somatic, social, and spiritual levels of experience.[71] In this respect, as will be seen later on, feelings have a special place in Epicurus' ethical concepts and in fact are to his Ethics what sensations are to his Physics: "It is the test of rightness in morals, that is, of rightness in action, just as sensation is the test of truth in knowledge, that is, of the rightness of apprehension." [72]

XVI   *Opposition and Praise*

The source of much controversy throughout the centuries, Epicurus' theories of the atoms, of sensation, and of knowledge have caused their propounder to be both reviled and revered. Inevitably he is scorned by those who hold to a transcendental theory of existence and who see in the atomist concept of life a glorification of materialism—the corporeal, the actual, the natural, the existential. The atomist, according to Jones, by declaring that life is no more than "a brief candle flickering for a moment in an immense dark," supports a pessimistic view that "the universe is a machine indifferent to us." Atomism, Jones continues, may have its occasional appeal, for "there are times when the world tastes like dust in the mouth." Still, he notes, atomism rejects all human hope by sacrificing it ultimately to the truth of things and to the world of external realities. "But since we must live," Jones concludes, "it is well that hope springs eternal. And just because hope does spring eternal, Atomism will seem unreal." [73]

In sharp contrast, Bertrand Russell admires the ancient atomists because they "asked the mechanistic question, and gave a mechanistic answer." Their successors in the Renaissance were more interested in the teleological question and thus "led science up a blind alley." Those who, along with Russell, praise atomists like Leucippus, Democritus, and Epicurus as being enlightened, respond to the attitude of these ancient thinkers because: "it was imaginative and vigorous and filled with the delight of adventure. They were interested in everything—meteors and eclipses, fishes and whirlwinds, religion and morality; with a penetrating intellect they combined the zest of children." [74] In the position taken by Russell, we can find a defense of the atomists not only because of their insistence on the superiority of physics over metaphysics but also because of their search for a "release from traditional hauntings." [75] Atomism to Russell is, as it were, a vindication of modernism over medievalism—an antidote against the "soaring poetries of Platonism and a Platonized Christianity," [76] to use the terminology of Strodach.

Who is right? Those counseling us "who are of the day, [to] be sober, putting on the breastplate of faith and love; and for an helmet, the hope of salvation"? [77] Or those who see the physical universe as containing the greatest adventures and the only true discoveries and who find their own real worth and meaning in being "engaged in a disinterested effort to understand the world"? [78] The answer, it seems, is as difficult as it is desperate. For the worlds of the "here" and of the "beyond" have from the earliest times alternately inspired and agonized man in quest of answers—and of consolation. For some the answer lies in lifelong hope and in eternity. For others the answer lies in understanding this world and in making peace with it. Epicurus is an eminent member of the latter group.

Yet it needs stressing, too, that if Epicurus preferred man to the divine, he also preferred man to science. "If our dread of the phenomena above us," he points out, "our fear lest death concern us, and our inability to discern the limits of pains and desires were not vexatious to us, we would have no need of the natural sciences." [79] The kingdom of heaven, he says, is to be found by man here and now. Moreover, it is to be found not in the speculative adventures either of mind or of spirit but in the attainment of imperturbability of both mind and spirit. By understanding his cosmos man can achieve this tranquillity. There is no special need, however, for man to triumph over this world by harnessing its powers. Understand the world, Epicurus says; don't exalt it, for then you would become its slave! And to be a slave of this world would be as disastrous as to be a slave of the world that some claim exists somewhere in the beyond.

In an astute essay, "Epicurus Relocated," Norman J. DeWitt has proposed a new relationship for Epicurus and his philosophy. The polarity, as DeWitt sees it, is not now necessarily between materialism and idealism, or between monism and pluralism. Rather, the polarity is between Aristotle and Epicurus: "between an organized environment and one of random, unpredictable events." As against Aristotle's "general theory of organization," "Epicurus was unable to justify universal organization by recourse to experience, and he appealed to the multitude of Greeks and Romans who were uneasy about administrators, human or divine. In fact it is not excessively clever to regard Epicurus as definitely *not* an Organization Man." [80]

The new relationship which DeWitt posits is really as old as the debate between those who contemplate Being and those who observe Becoming. In participating so fearlessly in this debate, which dates back to the beginning of human thought, Epicurus chose freedom over organization—freedom, above all, because it is the "greatest fruit of self-sufficiency." [81] His choice, it can be said, is at once an affirmation of man and an inspiration of hope itself.

CHAPTER 3

Cosmology

ORIGINALLY Epicurus presented his theories relating to the universe (*to pan*), the worlds (*kosmoi*), and the heavens (*meteōra*) in an important work, *On Nature.* Although this work has been lost, it is possible to reconstruct his cosmology on the basis of his extant writings, especially his *Letter to Pythocles,* in its entirety, and his *Letter to Herodotus,* in parts. Various sections of Lucretius' *On the Nature of Things* are also very helpful, particularly Books V and VI. Indeed, no account of Epicurus' cosmology can avoid a constant dependence on Lucretius.

Although generally regarded as the work of a compiler, the letter to Pythocles is considered an authoritative Epicurean text. The letter to Herodotus, described by Epicurus as a "brief compendium of the chief principles of my teaching as a whole," is often referred to as *The Lesser* or *The Minor Epitome*. It was written to refresh the minds of students who had already mastered the Epicurean system. On the other hand, *The Major Epitome*, which Lucretius obviously consulted for his poem, was a work for beginning students and contained a condensation of *On Nature*. Unfortunately, it too is now lost except for a few fragments discovered at Herculaneum.

I *The Rejection of Teleology*

Perhaps the most emphatic point made by Epicurus, explicitly or implicitly, is his rejection of the teleological view of nature, which is to say, the belief that natural phenomena are determined by an over-all design or purpose in nature, by divine grace, or by a divine artificer, a demiurge, an overlord. In this respect one must always bear in mind both Epicurus' theology and his impelling ethical concern with achieving peace of mind and happiness. At every step of the way Epicurus' cosmology must be approached in the light of his ceaseless attempts to teach man to overcome the bondage of religion, to get rid of superstition, to master the fear of death and of gods.

Lucretius points out that the imperfections of the world prove that it was not divinely created or ordered. As examples of these imperfections, he observes that vast tracts of the earth are made useless for man by wild beasts inhabiting mountains and forests, by rocks and bodies of water covering great spaces, and by the burning heat and the biting frost. "What is left for tillage," he continues, "even that nature by its power would overrun with thorns, unless the force of man made head against it, accustomed for the sake of a livelihood to groan beneath the strong hoe and to cut through the earth by pressing down the plough." [1]

According to Lucretius, an Epicurean must accept the fact that the natural world is mortal, subject as it is to diseases which come in all seasons of the year, to death which stalks all life, and to the recurring rhythm of creation and destruction. In short, the world must be conceived as a mortal body which has a beginning and an end. Following Epicurus' recommendation that we should express opinions, investigations, and problems in clear and exact terms, not "empty phrases," Lucretius then goes on to cite specific proofs of the earth's mortality. Thus, for instance, some part of the earth flies away in clouds of dust, after being "burnt up by constant suns, [and] trampled by a multitude of feet." [2] Another part of the earth "is put under water by rains, and rivers graze against and eat into the banks." The earth, in the final analysis, is not only the universal mother but also the "universal tomb." After indicating that the elements of water and air and fire are mortal, Lucretius declares that the strongest things themselves are mortal as well:

. . . even stones are conquered by time, . . . high towers fall and rocks moulder away, . . . shrines and idols of gods are worn out with decay, . . . the holy divinity cannot prolong the bounds of fate or struggle against the fixed laws of nature. . . . basalt rocks tumble down riven away from high mountains . . . unable to endure and suffer the strong might of finite age.[3]

In teaching that the natural world has no arbitrary, divine design, Epicurus echoed the earlier atomist philosophers like Leucippus and Democritus, though he evidently had "a greater unity of conception than can be extracted from the scattered testimonies to the theories" [4] of his predecessors. Like his philosophy as a whole, Epicurus' cosmology is tied to his materialism and to his uncompromising belief that man must at all times rely on the immediate and observable evidence of phenomena. Naturalistic principles of explanation, not theological dogmas or scientific hypotheses or mathematical theories, constituted for Epicurus the only bases of reality and truth. This aspect of Epicurus' thought, as characterized by his absolute reliance on the sensible and the material, on immediate consciousness, as it were, helps to explain why he taught his followers to concentrate on the real world and to consider as dangerous the abstractions of logic, rhetoric, and mathematics. (Cicero charged that as far as logic went, Epicurus was *inermis ac nudus,* that is, unarmed and naked!)[5]

It is of interest that Epicurus spurned literature, "the deadly bait of fiction," as he termed it, warning that the true philosopher must be wary of the ideas of the poets, who he believed are not concerned with securing empirical verification but with expressing emotional and esthetic values. Because of this distaste for literature, as De Lacy has indicated, Epicurus sought to use simple prose, not allegories and metaphors, prose that avoids the obscurities of rhetoric and transcends emotions in the pursuit of truth and of cognitive values.[6] Epicurus did not deign to rely on the graces of style but rather put his trust in the language of ordinary life, in what is plain and intelligible, free from superfluous literary adornments. The wise man, he believed, "will leave written words behind him, but will not compose panegyric." [7]

II *The Nature of the World*

Because atoms and space are infinite, the number of worlds, like and unlike our own, is infinite. "There nowhere exists an obstacle to the infinite number of the worlds," [8] in so far as the infinite number of atoms move through the greatest distances and the atoms appropriate to the creation and the maintenance of a world have not been used up on one world or on a limited number of worlds, whether like our own or different from it. Epicurus defines a world, it should be noted, as a certain limited part of the universe which "includes a sun, moon, stars, an earth, and all that occurs in the heavens; at its dissolution everything in it will be thrown into disorder. It is a segment of infinite space and terminates in a periphery that is either rarefied or dense, either in circular motion or in a state of rest, either spherical or triangular or of any other shape." [9] Such a world, Epicurus further observes, may be generated within a world or in the spaces between worlds: in a region for the most part empty, but not in a pure vacuum. The birth of such a world takes place "after the necessary atoms have streamed in from one or more worlds or interspaces, gradually form organized aggregates, and effect the transfer of matter to various areas of the system as chance dictates, feeding in the appropriate materials until the world is completed." [10] The worlds, moreover, have been generated from the infinite, each of them disengaging itself from its own whirling mass. We may assume that in these worlds, which are subject to deterioration by the changing of their parts, there are animals, plants, and the other things which we know in our own. Indeed, Epicurus contends, "no one could prove that in a world of one kind there might or might not have been included the kinds of seeds from which living things and plants and all the rest of the things we see are composed, and that in a world of another kind they could not have been." [11]

As is so often the case, Lucretius helps to clarify Epicurus' concept. He describes how the first atoms gathered together in a wild storm. "Then next," he continues, "the several parts began to fly asunder and things to be joined like with like and to mark off the world and portion out its members and arrange its mighty parts, . . . to separate high heaven from earth, and let the sea spread itself out apart with its unmixed water, and likewise let the fires of ether spread apart pure and unmixed." [12] After his account of the separation of the parts of the world, Lucretius shows how the heavier bodies of earth "met together in the middle and took up all of them the lowest positions." Now they squeezed out the light particles which were to make up the sea, the stars, the sun, the moon, and the walls of the world. Slowly each body took on a distinct shape: sun, moon, and stars now composed the heavens ("they were neither heavy enough to sink and settle down nor light enough to glide along the uppermost borders"). The earth, on the other hand, sank in the middle and formed the sea, but the mountains were left standing. In a passage summarizing this process, Lucretius is able to achieve in poetry what Epicurus could never do in prose:

Thus then the ponderous mass of earth was formed with close-cohering body and all the slime of the world . . . slid down by its weight to the lowest point and settled at the bottom like dregs. Then the sea, then the air, then the fire-laden ether itself, all are left unmixed with their clear bodies; and some are lighter than others, and clearest and lightest of all ether floats upon the airy currents, and blends not its clear body with the troubled airs; it suffers all these things below to be upset with furious hurricanes, suffers them to be troubled by wayward storms; while it carries along its own fires gliding with a changeless onward sweep. For that ether may stream on gently and with one uniform effort the Pontos shows, a sea which streams with a changeless current, ever preserving one uniform gliding course.[13]

That the world was not formed by some divine design but by the concourse of atoms is the cosmological theory most underscored by Epicurus' followers. Lucretius plainly makes this point in the following passage:

For verily not by design did the first-beginnings of things station themselves each in its right place guided by keen intelligence, nor did they bargain . . . what motions each should assume, but because many in number and shifting about in many ways throughout the universe they are driven and tormented by blows during infinite time past, after trying motions and unions of every kind at length they fall into arrangements such as those out of which this our sum of things has been formed, and by which too it is preserved through many great years when once it has been thrown into the appropriate motions, and causes the streams to replenish the greedy sea with copious river waters and the earth, fostered by the heat of the sun, to renew its produce, and the race of living things to come up and flourish, and the gliding fires of ether to live: all which these several things could in no wise bring to pass, unless a store of matter could rise up from infinite space, out of which store they are wont to make up in due season whatever has been lost.[14]

Elaborating further upon Epicurus' concept that nature works of itself, free from any divine control, Lucretius discusses the principle of growth and decay in life, a principle that Epicurus earlier had derived from Democritus. The Roman poet thus provides a picture of the Epicurean belief that in all bodies there is a period of growth when nature, "parent of things, with finishing hand has brought all things on to their utmost limit of growth," followed by a period of decay, when "piece by piece age breaks their powers.

and matured strength and wastes away on the side of decay." [15] The world itself, Lucretius insists, cannot escape the ravages that come with advanced age: "the walls too of the great world around shall be stormed and fall to decay and crumbling ruin." [16] It was, to be sure, "no golden chain let down to earth from heaven above the races of mortal beings . . . ," Lucretius adds, "but the same earth bare them which now feeds them out of herself." "All things are gradually wasting away and passing to the grave, quite forspent by age and length of days." [17] This is a truth which is at the heart of the meaning of all experience and of all existence for the Epicureans.

III   *The Development of Life*

The Epicurean concept of the development of culture, though briefly alluded to by Epicurus in his *Letter to Herodotus,* in which he characteristically specifies that instinct led man to the first developments "and that later on reasoning elaborated what had been suggested by nature and made further inventions," [18] is traced in graphic detail by Lucretius in Book V of his poem. He begins by going back to "the infancy of the world and the tender age of the fields of earth." [19] Emphasizing the role of mother earth as the producer of all things, Lucretius writes:

As feathers and hairs and bristles are first born on the limbs of four-footed beasts and the body of the strong of wing, thus the new earth then first put forth grass and bushes, and next gave birth to the races of mortal creatures springing up many in number in many ways after divers fashions. For no living creatures can have dropped from heaven nor can those belonging to the land have come out of the salt pools.[20]

Anticipating Darwin's theory of the survival of the fittest, he shows how nature at first created many deformed creatures (though he rejects the existence of monsters like centaurs, scyllas, and chimeras, as described in myth and legend) without feet, hands, mouths, or eyes—creatures that could neither propagate nor survive, lacking as they did craft or courage or speed, qualities essential to the protection and preservation of a race. "But those to whom nature has granted none of these qualities, so that they could neither live by their own means nor perform for us any useful service in return for which we should suffer their kind to feed and be safe under our protection, those . . . would lie exposed as a prey and booty of others, hampered all in their own death-bringing shackles, until nature brought that kind to utter destruction." [21]

Primitive man, in contrast, was both hardy and long-lived, "built on a groundwork of larger and more solid bones within, knit with powerful sinews throughout the frame of flesh; not lightly to be disabled by heat or cold or strange kinds of food or any malady of the body." [22] At first man did not till the earth but lived on the fruits of trees and drank from streams. Nor did he have clothing or houses, but dwelled in woods and in mountain caves and forests in order to avoid buffeting winds and heavy rains. Nor was he subject to customs or laws, or concerned with the general human welfare. "Whatever prize fortune threw in his way, each man would bear off, trained at his own discretion to think of himself and live for himself alone." [23] This primitive man, Lucretius declares, did not fear the darkness so much as the attacks of wild beasts. Thousands, of course, became the victims of beasts in those early days; yet, "then a single day gave not over to death many thousands of men marching with banners spread, nor did the stormy waters of the sea dash on the rocks men and ships." [24] Obviously, too, many men of primitive times died for want of food, but "now on the contrary 'tis plenty sinks into ruin." And unwittingly they would poison themselves, but "now with nicer skill men give it to their son's wife instead." [25] Slowly, therefore, "mankind began to soften" as primitive man acquired huts and skins and fire, learned the duties of wedlock, gave birth to offspring, and accepted the benefits of fire, clothing, and shelter. Soon men formed friendships, "desiring neither to do nor to suffer harm."

IV *The Origin of Language*

The naturalistic principles in both Epicurus and Lucretius are also seen in their theories of the origin of language. In the beginning, they thought, words did not receive meanings by design; nor were the names of things created by convention. On the contrary, Epicurus declares, the various ethnic groups, "on experiencing their own peculiar emotions and sensory impressions, uttered sounds conforming to these various emotions and impressions, each in its own way, corresponding to the geographical differences of the groups." [26] Later on these ethnic groups by common agreement gave particular names to particular sounds so as to make their meanings and intentions understandable and concise. It is worth noting that Lucretius took up only the first stage of the development of language, that is, the evolution of language naturally and spontaneously, whereas Epicurus accepted the later and deliberate role of reason in language as well as conventions which helped to "standardize both the structure of languages and the meanings of words." [27] "Sometimes," explains Epicurus, " . . . persons were forced to invent natural sounds for the objects; at other times they chose the sounds by a rational process in conformance with ordinary conventions, thereby clarifying their meaning." [28]

V *The Rise of Civilized Communities*

Depicting the rise of civilized communities, Lucretius shows how strong monarchs built fortresses and towns and divided lands among men according to their personal merits. Alas, but the discovery of gold altered the primordial standards of personal beauty, strength, and intellect in respect to the division of land and of wealth among men. Then, in words that take us back to Epicurus' most cherished counsel, Lucretius observes that "a frugal subsistence" and "a contented mind" comprise the truest riches, rather than wealth and ambition, which are the offshoots of false values and which inevitably lead to ruination:

But men desired to be famous and powerful, in order that their fortunes might rest on a firm foundation and they might be able by their wealth to lead a tranquil life; but in vain, since in their struggle to mount up to the highest dignities they rendered their path one full of danger; and even if they reach it, yet envy like a thunderbolt sometimes strikes and dashes men down from the highest point with ignominy into noisome Tartarus; since the highest summits and those elevated above the level of other things are mostly blasted by envy as by a thunderbolt; so that far better it is to obey in peace and quiet than to wish to rule with power supreme and be the master of kingdoms.[29]

He goes on to describe the development of law from its utilitarian basis, the origin of belief in the gods, the evolution of metalworking, the discovery of methods of warfare, the rise of the art of weaving, and the development of agricultural methods by which man forced "the forests to recede every day higher and higher up the hill-side and yield the ground below to tilth." [30]

In the remaining section of his account of the rise of civilization, Lucretius turns his attention to the origin of music. He shows how primitive man first imitated the notes of birds and of the wind in the reeds, and "learned sweet plaintive ditties, which the pipe pours forth pressed by the fingers of the players, heard through pathless woods and forests and lawns, through the unfrequented haunts of shepherds and abodes of unearthly calm." [31] Doubtless this part of his poem seeks to evoke the pleasures of conviviality which to an Epicurean are a means to happiness. In the following passage we find a vision of felicity:

Then went round the jest, the tale, the peals of merry laughter; for the peasant muse was then in its glory; then frolick mirth would prompt to entwine head and shoulders with garlands plaited with flowers and leaves, and to advance in the dance out of step and move the limbs clumsily and with clumsy foot beat mother earth; which would occasion smiles and peals of merry laughter, because all these things then from their greater novelty and strangeness were in high repute.[32]

But with a sense of disappointment Lucretius shows how in time distaste set in and old ways and simple joys were gradually despised and rejected by man. Now, Lucretius laments, man "ever toils vainly and to no purpose and wastes life in groundless cares" for gold and purple. Ambition and greed hold sway. Man has not learned "what is the true end of getting and up to what point genuine pleasure goes on increasing: this by slow degrees has carried life out into the deep sea and stirred up from their lowest depths the mighty billows of war." [33] Still, Lucretius feels, life goes on, the seasons come round, and work is carried on "after a fixed plan and fixed order":

Ships and tillage, walls, laws, arms, roads, dress, and all such like things, all the prizes, all the elegancies too of life without exception, poems, pictures, and the chiselling of fine-wrought statues, all these things practiced together with the acquired knowledge of the untiring mind taught men by slow degrees as they advanced on the way step by step.[34]

In affirming both the need for and the triumph of the enlightened mind, Lucretius also gives witness to the Epicurean belief that "time by degrees brings each several thing forth before men's eyes and reason raises it up into the borders of light." Experience gives birth to all inventions and to progress, and man ever utilizes his natural endowment—"for things must be brought to light one after the other and in due order in the different arts, until these have reached their highest point of development." [35]

VI *Cosmological Theories and Explanations*

Now when we come to the last phase of the discussion of Epicurus' cosmology, his concepts of the heavenly bodies and of astronomical and meteorological phenomena, we see a continuing emphasis on the fact that natural laws govern the universe. Any suggestion that a divinity inheres in and directs the heavenly bodies is categorically dismissed. Careful, too, to rule out any belief that heavenly bodies play a role in man's fortunes, Epicurus avers "that it is the task of natural science to determine with precision the causes of the most important phenomena and that our happiness is bound up with causal knowledge of the heavenly bodies, *i.e.*, with the understanding of the nature of celestial phenomena, and everything else that is germane to scientific knowledge relating to human happiness." [36] The study of celestial phenomena, moreover, has but one central purpose: the acquisition of mental composure and self-reliance.

Epicurus also points out that we must not force explanations of these phenomena, lest we make our treatment similar "to an explication of the problems of noncelestial physics [*e.g.*, terrestrial physics, metaphysics, and ethics]—as seen, for example, in the statements 'The universe consists of bodies and an intangible substance' or 'Atoms are indivisible' and in all other such cases where there is but a single explanation that is consistent with phenomena." [37] In short, Epicurus warns that the single causation theory of the atomist system, which he uses as the basis of his *Letter to Herodotus*, must not be used in the explanation of celestial bodies (sun, moon, stars) and movements (eclipses, risings, settings, etc.), for their origins have a plurality of causes, "and there is more than one set of predications relating to their nature that is compatible with our sensory experience." [38] Any failure to acquire infallible knowledge of particular causes of celestial phenomena need not disturb one, provided he possesses a general theory of causation. "Accordingly," Epicurus states, "if we suppose that it is possible for an event to take place in one particular way, under conditions where it is equally possible for us to feel unconcerned if we recognize that it may have more than one cause, we shall feel as undisturbed as if we knew that it occurs in one particular way." [39]

Epicurus clearly explains his theory of multiple causation in the area of celestial phenomena in his *Letter to Pythocles*. Throughout, his explanations are motivated by a steadfast wish to dramatize the fact that there is no god-controlled universe: "The gods must not be drawn into the discussion in any way, but must be left free from duties and in perfect blessedness." [40] The sun, the moon, and the other heavenly bodies were not formed by themselves and later drawn into the world, but rather they were formed along with it from the very first, "augmented by the conjunctions of swirling masses composed of tiny particles having the nature of air or fire or both." [41] The size of these celestial bodies, Epicurus notes, is approximately what our senses indicate, either somewhat greater than what we see or somewhat smaller or the same, for "this is the way that fiery objects on earth appear to the senses when viewed from a distance." [42]

Lucretius, in amplifying Epicurus' hypothesis, writes: "For from whatever distances fires can reach us with their light and breathe on our limbs burning heat, those distances take away nothing by such spaces between from the body of the flames, the fire is not in the least narrowed in appearance." [43] The motions of these bodies, the risings and settings of the sun, the moon, and the other heavenly bodies, may come about in various equally possible ways: *e.g.*, by "the lighting up and quenching of their fires"; by "the emergence of these bodies from a point above the earth and again by the earth's position in front of them"; by "the rotation of the heavens as a whole"; by "the slanting of the sky, which is forced into this position by the seasons"; by "transverse air currents"; by "the right sort of fuel [which] is always ignited in due order as the previous supply leaves off burning." [44]

The alternating phases of the moon, Epicurus explains, result from various causes: from its own rotation, "from the configuration of the air," or from some other body which places itself in front of the moon. Possibly the moon has its own light, and possibly its light comes from the sun, for "in our own experience we observe many objects that have their own light and many that get light from other sources." [45] The apparent face in the moon, Epicurus ventures, may be caused by variations of its physical features, its surface, or by some object in front of it. As to the eclipses of the sun or the moon, he gives as possible causes the extinction of their fires and the interposition of other bodies, such as the earth or some invisible body. Elucidating then the varying lengths of night and day, he cites the sun's movements over the earth, as "it crosses areas of varying length or passes over certain areas more rapidly than others." [46]

VII *Meteorological, Atmospheric, and Terrestrial Phenomena*

After giving his theories relating to the heavenly bodies, Epicurus examines meteorological phenomena. Clouds, he says, are formed by the compression of air or by the gathering of moisture. Rain is caused when clouds are compressed or there is "the downflow of winds moving through the atmosphere out of the right quarter." [47] Thunder is caused by wind within the clouds or by the rending or friction of clouds. Lightning, which Epicurus conceives of as preceding thunder because it causes thunder, results when the proper atoms escape from the clouds, when fire from the stars falls from the clouds where it has gathered, when fire-producing atoms set clouds on fire, or when winds or clouds under pressure burst into flame. A thunderbolt, that is, "lightning that strikes," is produced when fire in the clouds cannot penetrate them and a part of it breaks through and "descends violently to the ground below." It is quite possible, he confesses, that thunderbolts may be caused in other ways as well. "Only let there be an end to mythologizing!" [48] he exhorts. Lucretius, in fact, devotes more than two hundred lines to attacking religious myths and superstitions connected with celestial phenomena. The thunderbolt in particular, he feels, is not the sign of divine wrath. Indeed, asks Lucretius, if it were, why would Jupiter strike the innocent and spare the guilty? Why expend his thunderbolts on "waste places"? Why "dash down the holy sanctuaries of the gods and his own gorgeous seats with the destroying thunderbolt, and break the finewrought idols of the gods, and spoil his own images of their glory by an overbearing wound?" [49]

Some of the other atmospheric and terrestrial phenomena and their possible causes, Epicurus continues, are cyclones, which occur when a cloud is rotated by the winds, or when a cloud enters a whirling wind, or when a wind "is generated and is unable to flow through the cloud mass sideways because of the compression of the atmosphere around it";[50] earthquakes, which are caused by the trapping of wind in the earth or by the diffusion "of the motion caused by the caving in of masses of earth and the countermotion that occurs when the former meets with thick concentrations of earth";[51] hail, which is caused by the process of heavy freezing or by a moderate freezing of water particles or of wind particles; and snow, which results from mist that is frozen as it falls from clouds or from "the friction of clouds that have assumed a frozen state." Dew is produced by particles of moisture and "by the evaporation of particles from damp spots or places containing water." [52] Ice is produced when the rough particles expel the smooth particles from water. The rainbow is produced by the sun shining on mist— or as it is depicted by Lucretius:

And rains are wont to hold out and to last long, when many seeds of water are stirred to action, and clouds upon clouds and rack upon rack welling forth from all quarters round about are borne along, and when the reeking earth steams moisture back again from its whole surface. When in such a case the sun has shone with his rays amid the murky tempest right opposite the dripping rain-clouds, then the colour of the rainbow shows itself among the black clouds.[53]

VIII   *Celestial Phenomena*

In his concluding section on celestial phenomena, Epicurus relates that the halo around the moon is formed when air is carried from every quarter toward the moon and either checks the currents of light which flow uniformly from the moon or "holds back the atmosphere around the moon symmetrically at every point, so as to spread it thickly in a circle." [54] Comets occur when fire is collected together in the upper air in certain regions and at certain periods; they are revealed to us by a movement of the sky, or they start to move because of special circumstances and "come into areas of the heavens over us and thus become visible." [55] Borrowing Homer's expression, Epicurus notes that certain stars "revolve in their place" because this part of the world is fixed, or because "a vortex of air encircles it, which is an impediment to their ranging about as the other stars do," or because they lack a necessary supply of fuel "except in this region of the sky where we see that they are fixed." [56]

That some of the stars are planets, or stars that wander in their courses, may be due to several causes, including the fact that necessity decreed this as they moved from the beginning, some rotating regularly and others irregularly. Differences in the velocity of certain stars may be caused in three ways: "because they move in the same circular orbit but rotate more slowly than the others," "because they move in the opposite direction but are held back by the revolution of the other stars," or "because all stars traverse the same circular path, but some rotate over a greater area, others over a lesser." [57] Falling stars may be produced in part by a collision of stars and the consequent falling out of fragments, by the meeting of atoms which produce fire, or by "a concourse of winds in dense, mistlike concentrations; this mass then ignites because of compression, bursts out of the surrounding matter, and falls toward whatever region its impetus carries it." [58]

IX *The Principle of Multiple Causation*

Referring to Epicurus' principle of multiple causation in dealing with heavenly phenomena, Strodach opines that in the *Letter to Pythocles* we have "a grab bag of ill-assorted and sometimes fantastic theories." [59] Still, it should be stressed that from Epicurus' standpoint nothing could be as fantastic as dogmatic theological explanations of the physical universe. Not only do celestial occurrences have more than one explanation that is in harmony with the evidence of the senses, but the theories about them are only probable. Indeed, Epicurus says, "if a person takes one explanation and throws out another that is equally compatible with the phenomenon, it is obvious that he is departing completely from scientific procedure and has slipped into religious superstition." [60] We must always hold to the "possible," therefore, in explaining heavenly phenomena and be "able to refer each theory to some phenomenal counterpart and not stand in awe of the slavish fabrications of the astronomers" [61] (*e.g.*, Aristotle and Eudoxus).

Returning again and again to those who would insist on a single cause, Epicurus believes that such persons "have failed to observe whether it is possible for human beings to use the empirical method." [62] But if one is to avoid mythologizing, he must bend every effort to "follow the evidence of the senses in gleaning hints about things unseen." [63] Consequently, to seek to apply the "one cause" method to celestial phenomena when the phenomena demand a grasp of multiple causation "is a mad and improper practice of persons who have espoused the worthless science of astrology and who reduce causal theory to meaninglessness when they fail to release the deity from such duties." [64] Such persons really "want to parade their superstitions before the mob." [65] Only when man has learned that there are various causes of celestial phenomena and of all the other occurrences that constantly take place, will he be able to liberate himself at last from "everything that drives other men to the extremes of fear" [66] and hence to achieve tranquillity and happiness.

CHAPTER 4

Theology

On Piety and *On the Gods* were the titles of two of Epicurus' most important works. Although these works have not come down to us, their basic contents are strongly hinted at in what Epicurus says about religious beliefs in his writings which have come down. Besides, there are valuable expositions of Epicurean theology in Lucretius' poem and in Cicero's treatise *On the Nature of the Gods,* which, together with fragments from Philodemus, make it possible for us to put together an account of Epicurus' religious attitudes. It must be recalled that Epicurus lived in a period of ostentatious religious displays: "Never had such rich gifts flowed into the temples. Never had there been so many festivals, games, processions, sacrifices, or votive offerings. Never had so many temples been built." [1] Perhaps the most significant quality of Epicurus' theology is his refusal to accept the popular religious notions of his time, specifically those relating to the gods and to death. Justifiably, he can be called one of history's earliest and bravest religious nonconformists and reformers.

In spite of his hagiographic tendencies, Lucretius is not far from the truth when he declares that it was Epicurus who ventured first to oppose "the evils to which religion could prompt." "Him neither story of gods nor thunderbolts nor heaven with threatening roar could quell," the Roman poet says; "they only chafed the more the eager courage of his soul, filling him with desire to be the first to burst the fast bars of nature's portals." [2] Epicurus is often pictured as a moralist who taught his disciples the saving values of self-sufficiency and of tranquillity of soul. That he was also a theologian is manifest in his pronouncements that the good and pious life is a life wholly removed from antiquated religious fears and superstitions, from "the dumb demands of man's infra-rational nature," [3] as it has been aptly put. To a large extent, Epicurus' was a theology of freedom, trying to dispel the terror of the darkness of mind.

Epicurus' *Letter to Menoeceus,* judged by classical scholars as the most polished and literary of his extant works, contains some of his finest religious sentiments. In it can be heard the voice of a master speaking to his disciple. Understanding, humility, reverence—these constitute the religious aspects of Epicurus' words and at the same time define his religious ideology, or what might better be called his religious humanism. For Epicurus, who was careful to distinguish between diverse pleasures, the good life is commensurate with the religious life. Furthermore, the ascetical life which he both recommended and sanctified anticipates with almost startling impact the asceticism preached by the great Christian teachers of later centuries.

I *The Religious Life*

In his delineation of the good life, that is, of the religious life, Epicurus assigned the highest place to prudence, which gives birth to all the other virtues. Of particular importance, as already seen, is his stress on man's freedom of choice, another of his teachings which invites comparison with those of Christianity. The deeply moral tone of these teachings is incontestable in Epicurus' belief that the prudent man knows not only the boundary lines of good and evil but also the ascendancy of man over Fate:

Of all this the beginning and the greatest good is prudence. Wherefore prudence is a more precious thing even than philosophy: for from prudence are sprung all the other virtues. . . . For indeed who, think you, is a better man than he who holds reverent opinions concerning the gods, and is at all times free from fear of death, and has reasoned out the end ordained by nature? He understands that the limit of good things is easy to fulfil and easy to attain, whereas the course of ills is either short in time or slight in pain: he laughs at destiny, whom some have introduced as the mistress of all things. He thinks that with us lies the chief power in determining events, some of which happen by necessity and some by chance, and some are within our control; for while necessity cannot be called to account, he sees that chance is inconstant, but that which is in our control is subject to no master, and to it are naturally attached praise and blame. For, indeed, it were better to follow the myths about the gods than to become a slave to the destiny of the natural philosophers: for the former suggests a hope of placating the gods by worship, whereas the latter involves a necessity which knows no placation.[4]

Nor did Epicurus visualize the life of the religious man to be complete without constant meditation upon the meaning of life. It is interesting to note that he advised his follower to meditate in company with a friend as well as alone, a fact reiterating the importance which he gave to fellowship. The state of feelings which Epicurus believed attendant upon the good life is that of piety, which sets one above other men:

Meditate therefore on these things and things akin to them night and day by yourself, and with a companion like to yourself, and never shall you be disturbed waking or asleep, but you shall live like a god among men. For a man who lives among immortal blessings is not like to a mortal being.[5]

II *Withdrawal from the World*

Naturally Epicurus' religious ideas, or contemplations, as they perhaps ought to be called, must be seen against the background of the violence and the militarism of Hellenistic times, when, in spite of religious displays, the old foundations of belief and conduct had deteriorated and a state of inward security was deeply desired. To achieve security, Epicurus averred, each man had to renounce the world around him, that is, to retreat from the workaday world and to conquer the fears and the desires that impede happiness. Doubtless there is basis for describing Epicurus' followers as a monastic community of "austere refined quietists." [6] And it is not at all farfetched to draw parallels between the life of withdrawal in Epicurus' garden and the life of prayer in Christian monastic communities of the Middle Ages, with the distinction that in the former the goal was a good life here and now, whereas in the latter the goal was eternal life in the world beyond.

To a large extent life in Epicurus' garden was characterized by intense spiritual awareness and discrimination, by the desire to escape contact with the outside world and the contaminations of human activity and to uphold the virtues of prudence and of humanity. Epicurus wanted his followers to concentrate on the inner life and on the religious and ethical elements that are implicit in this life. In contrast with both Plato and Aristotle, Epicurus believed that the contemplative life could be achieved in this world, not in some celestial city.

III *Astral Religion*

In his efforts to escape the multiplying contemporary beliefs in occult forces that found expression in astrology, magic, and superstition, Epicurus vehemently repudiated any belief in astral religion. His repudiation can be interpreted as an answer to the religious thinkers who said that the motions of the heavenly bodies are controlled by astral deities such as those, for instance, who are discussed by Plato in his *Timaeus, Laws,* and *Epinomis.* Epicurus' theology can be said to have been inspired by his opposition to Platonic idealism in general and to Plato's astral religion in particular, which is embodied in a passage like the following:

For mankind it should have been proof that the stars and their whole procession have intelligence, that they act with unbroken uniformity, because their action carries out a plan resolved on from untold ages; they do not change their purpose confusedly, acting now thus, and again thus, and wandering from one orbit to another. Yet most of us have imagined the very opposite; because they act with uniformity and regularity, we fancy them to have no souls. Hence the mass has followed the leading of fools; it imagines that man is intelligent and alive because he is so mutable, but deity, because it keeps to the same orbits, is unintelligent. Yet man might have chosen the fairer, better, more welcome interpretation; he might have understood that that which eternally does the same acts, in uniform way and for the same reasons, is for that very reason to be deemed intelligent, and that this is the case with the stars; they are the fairest of all sights to the eye, and as they move through the figures of the fairest and most glorious of dances they accomplish their duty to all living creatures. And for further proof that we have the right to ascribe souls to them, let us, in the first place, but think of their magnitude. . . . So let us but consider how anything can be made to cause so vast a bulk to revolve perpetually in the same period, as the stars in fact revolve. Why, I say, God will be found to be the cause; the thing is impossible on other terms, for . . . soul can be imparted by God, and by God alone. And since God has this power, 'tis perfectly easy for him first to give life to any body or any bulk, and then to set it moving as He judges best.[7]

Because the fear of unseen powers was especially repugnant to him, Epicurus was uncompromising in his attacks not only on false religion but also on false science. No divinity directs celestial phenomena, nor are these phenomena divine, Epicurus maintains, in words that must be seen as a direct assault on Plato's astral theories as quoted above:

Furthermore, the motions of the heavenly bodies and their turnings and eclipses and risings and settings, and kindred phenomena to these, must not be thought to be due to any being who controls and ordains or has ordained them and at the same time enjoys perfect bliss together with immortality (for trouble and care and anger and kindness are not consistent with a life of blessedness, but these things come to pass where there is weakness and fear and dependence on neighbours). Nor again must we believe that they, which are but fire agglomerated in a mass, possess blessedness, and voluntarily take upon themselves these movements.[8]

An important task, then, was to emphasize that there is no divine interference in the world. It is in the *Letters* to Herodotus and to Pythocles (as well as in Books V and VI of Lucretius' poem) that we encounter Epicurus' "beliefs in regard to things above the earth." In his attempts to exclude any possible divine interference in the world and to affirm that the sole object to be gained from a knowledge of celestial phenomena is "peace of mind and a sure confidence," Epicurus insists that things above us "admit of more than one cause of coming into being and more than one account of their nature which harmonizes with our sensations."[9] His opposition to any divine artificer or intelligence determining the motions of celestial phenomena and the destiny of human life must also be viewed in the framework of his opposition to the powers and the decrees of Fate. A wise man, he says, does not regard chance

as a god as most men do (for in a god's acts there is no disorder), nor as an uncertain cause of all things: for he does not believe that good and evil are given by chance to man for the framing of a blessed life, but that opportunities for great good and great evil are afforded by it. He therefore thinks it better to be unfortunate in reasonable action than to prosper in unreason. For it is better in a man's actions that what is well chosen should fail, rather than that what is ill chosen should be successful owing to chance.[10]

Returning always to the premise that tranquillity of soul may be ever disturbed by the presence of fears, Epicurus brings out that disturbances arise because man is "always expecting or imagining some everlasting misery, such as is depicted in legends, or [he fears] even . . . the loss of feeling in death." [11] But these fears, states Epicurus, are groundless, caused as they are not by a reasoned opinion but by an irrational imagination which ascribes no limits to the suffering of the "hapless race of men." Tranquillity, though, is not altogether elusive; these fears that create turmoil can be vanquished. Tranquillity will come about if only man trusts to his immediate feelings and sensations, to facts, for by heeding these he will be able to trace the causes of mental disturbances. (At the same time Epicurus dismisses any idea of divination. "Prophecy does not exist," he states, "and even if it did exist, things that come to pass must be counted nothing to us.")[12] When man has learned the real causes of celestial phenomena and all other incidental occurrences, he will be free "from all which produces the utmost fear in other men." It is this knowledge which in turn leads to piety, consisting not in external forms of worship but in the attitude that Lucretius describes in these words:

No act is it of piety to be often seen with veiled head to turn to a stone and approach every altar and fall prostrate on the ground and spread out the palms before the statues of the gods and sprinkle the altars with much blood of beasts and link vow on to vow, but rather to be able to look on all things with a mind at peace.[13]

IV *The Gods*

By no means did Epicurus deny the existence of gods, about whom, Lucretius appropriately tells us, "he was wont to deliver many precepts in beautiful and godlike phrase." At the beginning of his *Letter to Menoeceus*, Epicurus comes quickly to the point by confessing his belief that the gods are incorruptible and blessed beings and that the acceptance of this principle will help to lead man to the good life. But at the same time he refuses to accept the popular conceptions of the gods:

For gods there are, since the knowledge of them is by clear vision. But they are not such as the many believe them to be: for indeed they do not consistently represent them as they believe them to be. And the impious man is not he who denies the gods of the many, but he who attaches to the gods the beliefs of the many. For the statements of the many about the gods are not conceptions derived from sensation, but false suppositions, according to which the greatest misfortunes befall the wicked and the greatest blessings the good by the gift of the gods.[14]

It is the fear of the absolute power and the erratic will of the gods that elicits Epicurus' disdain—the same fear that Lucretius pictures as gaining "an entry into men's breasts, and now throughout the world maintains as holy fanes, lakes, groves, altars, and idols of the gods." [15] Indeed, Velleius, the Epicurean exponent in Cicero's dialogue *On the Nature of the Gods,* does not hesitate to say that anyone who ponders Epicurus' theology ought to regard him "with reverence, and to rank him as one of the very gods about whom we are inquiring." In a sweeping refutation of the theological beliefs of the philosophical school from Thales downward— beliefs which he feels "are more like the dreams of madmen than the considered opinions of philosophers"—Velleius claims that many philosophers' opinions as to the nature of the gods are "baseless and irrational," but "little less absurd" than those of the earliest poets of antiquity, who

have represented the gods as inflamed by anger and maddened by lust, and have displayed to our gaze their wars and battles, their fights and wounds, their hatreds, enmities and quarrels, their births and deaths, their complaints and lamentations, the utter and unbridled licence of their passions, their adulteries and imprisonments, their unions with human beings and the birth of mortal progeny from an immortal parent.[16]

Man's knowledge of the gods, Epicurus believed, is imprinted in the mind by nature. Their existence, as we read in Cicero's dialogue, "is therefore a necessary inference, since we possess an instinctive or rather an innate concept of them." [17] It was Epicurus' opinion that this "innate" concept of the eternal and blessed gods is universal. Moreover, the gods are not apprehended as physical entities, for, as Lucretius stipulates, "the fine nature of the gods far withdrawn from our senses is hardly seen by the thought of the mind; and since it has ever eluded the touch and stroke of the hands, it must touch nothing which is tangible for us; for that cannot touch which does not admit of being touched in turn." [18] Rather, the gods are perceived by "images" (*eidola*) which ceaselessly float down from interstellar space into the receptive minds of the pious. It is Lucretius once more who describes the "glorious forms" of these anthropomorphic images visiting men "in waking mind" and "in sleep." To these images men

would attribute sense, because they seemed to move their limbs and to utter lofty words suitable to their glorious aspect and surpassing powers. And they would give them life everlasting, because their face would ever appear before them and their form abide; yes and yet without all this, because they would not believe that beings possessed of such powers could lightly be overcome by any force. And they would believe them to be preeminent in bliss, because none of them was ever troubled with the fear of death, and because at the same time in sleep they would see them perform many miracles, yet feel on their part no fatigue from the effort.[19]

Epicurus' gods are a part of the natural order of the living universe. They have human shape, we are informed in Cicero's dialogue, for "what shape or outline can be more beautiful than the human form?" Yet, his gods are at the top of the scale of nature, for "if the human figure surpasses the form of all other living beings, and [a] god is a living being, [a] god must possess the shape which is the most beautiful of all." (Indeed, "their form is not corporeal, but only resembles bodily substance; it does not contain blood, but the semblance of blood.")[20] These gods are innumerable, and they live in the *intermundia* (or *metakosmia*), that is, the spaces between worlds.

Extending this speculation, as reported by Cicero, Epicurus originated a principle of infinity according to which in the universe "everything has its exact match and counterpart," a principle which, it is believed, Epicurus termed *isonomia*. "From this principle," we read in *On the Nature of the Gods*, "it follows that if the whole number of mortals be so many, there must exist no less a number of immortals, and if the causes of destruction are beyond count, the causes of conservation also are bound to be infinite." [21] Noting that Epicurus' principle of infinity recognized perfection and imperfection alike, DeWitt points out that Epicurus' *isonomia* should be translated as "equitable apportionment" and not as "equal distribution." "It does not denote balance or equilibrium," DeWitt argues. "No two sets of similar forces are in balance; in the individual world the forces of destruction always prevail at last, and in the universe at large the forces of preservation prevail at all times." [22]

V *The* Intermundia

In the *intermundia*, inhabited by the gods, the forces of creation and preservation are both superior and infinite. The abodes of the gods, like their special worlds, are not comparable to human abodes, but "fine, even as their bodies are." Consequently, into these abodes as into the gods themselves, Bailey brings out, "there never enter . . . the alien and fatal elements." [23] Here, Epicurus stresses, the gods live a life free "from the burdensome duties and in entire blessedness." Borrowing from the *Odyssey*, Lucretius pictures the gods' dwelling place as one which "neither winds do shake nor clouds drench with rains nor snow congealed by sharp frosts harms with hoary fall: an ever cloudless ether o'er-canopies them, and they laugh with light shed largely round." [24] (Philodemus went so far as to claim that Epicurus' gods conversed in Greek!)

The existence and the nature of the gods signify above all else a perfect and untroubled life, the supreme blessing of *ataraxia:* a world without wars, without generals, without Alexanders, without political leaders, orators, and prophets—without anything that disturbs peace of mind. "The blessed and immortal nature," Epicurus states in the first of the *Principal Doctrines,* "knows no trouble itself nor causes trouble to any other, so that it is never constrained by anger or favour. For all such things exist only in the weak." A god, thus, achieves a perfection beyond perfection; his life is "the happiest conceivable, and the one most bountifully furnished with all good things. . . . he toils not neither does he labour, but he takes delight in his own wisdom and virtue, and knows with absolute certainty that he will always enjoy pleasures at once consummate and everlasting." [25]

VI *Worship*

Worship the gods, do not fear them—these words best summarize Epicurus' attitude. By worshiping the gods, man but seeks to emulate them and then to imbue his own life with repose, freedom, and happiness. The function, therefore, of Epicurus' gods is ethical, in so far as they are "the paragons of the good life" who "create no trouble for themselves and seek to cause none to others." [26] A good man has a profound need for the gods, for they alone personify the virtues and the wisdom that can alleviate human misery. Philodemus notes, in fact, that Epicurus "calls the wise the friends of the gods and the gods the friends of the wise." [27] But the gods do not trouble themselves with the affairs of men, which might compromise their tranquillity. If the gods listened to the prayers of bad men, Epicurus is reported to have said, "all men would quickly have perished: for they are forever praying for evil against one another." [28] Divine perfection is not concerned with the contemplation of mortal imperfection. The infallible have no time for the fallible. The gods do not bestow gifts; neither do they need man's gifts, for they enjoy the greatest gift of all—serenity of soul:

For what advantage [Lucretius says to Memmius] can our gratitude bestow on immortal and blessed beings, that for our sakes they should take in hand to administer aught? And what novel incident should have induced them hitherto at rest so long after to desire to change their former life? For it seems natural he should rejoice in a new state of things, whom old things annoy; but for him whom no ill has befallen in times gone by, when he passed a pleasant existence, what could have kindled in such a one a love of change? [29]

By worshiping the gods, then, Epicurus meant that a good man, in contrast to an evil man, partakes of their unexcelled joys and blessedness. For this reason he encouraged his followers to observe traditional religious festivals and to "sacrifice piously and rightly where it is customary," for on these sacred occasions, moments of relief from the routine of life, men share in the everlasting happiness enjoyed by the gods. Epicurus reputedly admitted that "though he destroyed providence, he left a place for piety." [30] Indeed, in a way not unlike that of Plato, Epicurus duly stressed the importance of contemplating divine beauty and "the measureless and boundless extent of space that stretches in every direction, into which when the mind projects and propels itself, it journeys onward far and wide without ever sighting any margin or ultimate point where it can stop." [31]

Yet his gods are by their very nature indifferent to the human scene. At best, they can be viewed as moral ideals for man to emulate; at worst, they are an elite who cannot be bothered with puny mankind. Undoubtedly, Epicurus did strike a blow against the idea of the tyranny of the gods—but at a price, according to Wallace, who writes: "The fear of God is thus removed, obviously at the price of losing the love of God also." [32] In any event, Epicurus' gods are "entirely inactive and free from all ties of occupation," in sharp contrast to the Stoic god, who seems to be "grievously overworked." That the gods achieve eternal happiness only when they are exempt from all duties related to governing the cosmos is shown by Cicero's Epicurean Velleius:

If the world itself is god, what can be less restful than to revolve at incredible speed round the axis of the heavens without a single moment of respite? but repose is an essential condition of happiness. If on the other hand some god resides within the world as its governor and pilot, maintaining the courses of the stars, the changes of the seasons and all the ordered process of creation, and keeping a watch on land and sea to guard the interests and lives of men, why, what a bondage of irksome and laborious business is his! [33]

VII *Death*

Like the fear of the gods, Epicurus accounted the fear of death as a major cause of human misery. This fear is nearly as universal as death itself. "It is possible to provide security against other ills," we read in one of the most eloquent of *The Vatican Sayings*, "but as far as death is concerned, we men all live in a city without walls." [34] Man, says Epicurus, can never overcome the fact of death, but he can overcome "the terror of the soul" which this fact causes. His approach to death constitutes one of the four principal "remedies" (*tetrapharmacon*) necessary to the well-being of man—"*Nothing to fear in God: Nothing to feel in Death: Good can be attained: Evil can be endured.*" [35] His concept of death fortified his followers and even influenced his opponents. For example, in their writings and sermons some of the Church Fathers and later preachers like, say, the French bishop, historian, and orator Jacques-Bénigne Bossuet (1627–1704) cryptically made use of Epicurean statements. In addition, we need only study Montaigne's essay "That to Philosophize Is to Learn to Die"—particularly a sentence like "To know how to die delivers us from all subjection and restraint"—to gauge the impact of Epicurus' concept of death on great thinkers even centuries after him. The reason for his influence on both followers and adversaries becomes obvious when we meditate on sayings like these:

We are born once and cannot be born twice, but for all time must be no more. But you, who are not master of to-morrow, postpone your happiness: life is wasted in procrastination and each one of us dies without allowing himself leisure.

Some men throughout their lives gather together the means of life, for they do not see that the draught swallowed by all of us at birth is a draught of death.[36]

By his writings and by his example, Epicurus sought to teach his followers not only how to die but how to win victory over the fear of death. This fear of death and of an afterlife bringing reward or punishment he saw as a major disturbance to the peace of mind of those who are "always expecting or imagining some everlasting misery, such as is depicted in legends, or even . . . the loss of feeling in death." In one of his fragments Epicurus shows the results of the fear of death: "Even if [men think] they are able to escape punishment, it is impossible to win security for escaping: and so the fear of the future which always presses upon them does not suffer them to be happy or to be free from anxiety in the present." [37] All this fear is groundless, says Epicurus. Man is born to die, but, he reasons, "Death is nothing to us: for that which is dissolved is without sensation; and that which lacks sensation is nothing to us." [38]

VIII *A Way of Death*

By far the most complete and the most stirring pronouncements on death made by Epicurus are those in his *Letter to Menoeceus*. One cannot read this gracious letter without realizing why Epicurus was revered as a saviour by his followers. His utterances constitute a way of death, as it were. "Become accustomed to the belief that death is nothing to us," Epicurus writes with a simplicity of language second only to his wisdom. A healthy, vital outlook impregnates his words, which serve as an answer to death in the recurring phrase "death is nothing to us" ("mēden pros hēmas einai ton thanaton"). The fear of death, the pain of death, the illusion of immortality—these have no place in Epicurus' way. Indeed, the occasion of someone else's death is one for meditation,

[78]

not lamentation, for glad remembrance of love and friendship, not grief, for "sweet is the memory of a dead friend." [39] On the prospect of one's own death, Epicurus' words to Menoeceus, which are worth quoting in full, manifest courage in the face of what Lucretius later speaks of as "that dread of Acheron . . . troubling as it does the life of man from its inmost depths and overspreading all things with the blackness of death, allowing no pleasure to be pure and unalloyed": [40]

For all good and evil consists in sensation, but death is deprivation of sensation. And therefore a right understanding that death is nothing to us makes the mortality of life enjoyable, not because it adds to it an infinite span of time, but because it takes away the craving for immortality. For there is nothing terrible in life for the man who has truly comprehended that there is nothing terrible in not living. So that the man speaks but idly who says that he fears death not because it will be painful when it comes, but because it is painful in anticipation. For that which gives no trouble when it comes, is but an empty pain in anticipation. So death, the most terrifying of ills, is nothing to us, since so long as we exist death is not with us; but when death comes, then we do not exist. It does not then concern either the living or the dead, since for the former it is not, and the latter are no more.

But the many at one moment shun death as the greatest of evils, at another yearn for it as a respite from the evils in life. But the wise man neither seeks to escape life nor fears the cessation of life, for neither does life offend him nor does the absence of life seem to be any evil. And just as with food he does not seek simply the larger share and nothing else, but rather the most pleasant, so he seeks to enjoy not the longest period of time, but the most pleasant.

And he who counsels the young man to live well, but the old man to make a good end, is foolish, not merely because of the desirability of life, but also because it is the same training which teaches to live well and to die well. Yet much worse still is the man who says it is good not to be born, but

'once born make haste to pass the gates of Death.'
For if he says this from conviction why does he not pass away out of life? For it is open to him to do so, if he had firmly made up his mind to this. But if he speaks in jest, his words are idle among men who cannot receive them.

We must then bear in mind that the future is neither ours, nor yet wholly not ours, so that we may not altogether expect it as sure to come, nor abandon hope of it, as if it will certainly not come. [41]

IX *"Hymn to Death"*

Lines 830–1094 of Book III, containing Lucretius' famous "Hymn to Death," are considered one of the most elevated and moving passages in ancient poetry. Beginning with "Death therefore is nothing to us; it concerns us not a jot" ("Nihil igitur mors est ad nos nesque pertinet"), which has a striking resemblance to Epicurus' repeated expression "Death is nothing for us," Lucretius goes on to assert that men will not be conscious after death any more than they were before birth:

thus when we shall be no more, when there shall have been a separation of body and soul, out of both of which we are each formed into a single being, to us, you may be sure, who then shall be no more, nothing whatever can happen to excite sensation, not if earth shall be mingled with sea and sea with heaven.[42]

Man should not be bitter, he continues, when he comes at last to "sleep and rest." In death, even more than in sleep, "no craving whatever for ourselves then moves us." Even the laws of nature and the cycle of life should inform man's response to death: "for old things give way and are supplanted by new without fail, and one thing must ever be replenished out of other things." Moreover, there is no hell in the mythical deeps of Acheron. Hell exists only in the terror of it, so that "the life of fools at length becomes a hell here on earth":[43]

No Tantalus, numbed by groundless terror, as the story is, fears poor wretch a huge stone hanging in air; but in life rather a baseless dread of the god vexes mortals: the fall they fear is such fall of luck as chance brings to each. Nor do birds eat a way into Tityos laid in Acheron, nor can they sooth to say find during eternity food to peck under his large breast. However huge the bulk of body he extends, though such as to take up with outspread limbs not nine acres merely, but the whole earth, yet will he not be able to endure everlasting pain and supply food from his own body for ever. But he is for us a Tityos, whom, as he grovels in love, vultures rend and bitter anguish eats up or troubled thoughts from any other passion do rive. In life too we have a Sisyphus before our eyes who is bent on asking from the people the rods and cruel axes, and always retires defeated and disappointed. . . . Moreover Cerberus and the furies and yon privation of light are idle tales, as well as all the rest, Ixion's wheel and black Tartarus belching forth hideous fires from his throat: things which nowhere are nor sooth to say can be. But there is in life a dread of punishment for evil deeds, signal as the deeds are signal, and for atonement of guilt, the prison and the frightful hurling down from the rock, scourgings, executioners, the dungeon of the doomed, the pitch, the metal plate, torches; and even though these are wanting, yet the conscience-stricken mind through boding fears applies to itself goads and frightens itself with whips, and sees not meanwhile what end there can be of ills or what limit at last is to be set to punishments, and fears lest these very evils be enhanced after death.[44]

The fear of death is folly, for death is the legacy of life. Kings of mighty empires, great heroes and warriors, poets, and philosophers cannot, with all their power and with all their wisdom, triumph over the everlasting fact that "a sure term of life is fixed for mortals, and death cannot be shunned." Lucretius' "Hymn to Death" concludes with the epitaphial words "for no less long a time will he be no more in being, who beginning with to-day has ended his life, than the man who has died many months and years ago." [45] These words evoke the quiet wisdom of Epicurus' reminder, "as far as death is concerned, we men all live in a city without walls."

X *An Age of Crisis and Mysticism*

Above all, Epicurus' religious concepts must be seen as developing in and reacting against an age when the struggle for power among Alexander's successors went on with increasing ferocity. Living then, said Eumenes, one of these successors, was like "living in a great herd of wild beasts." [46] Such an age must have convinced Epicurus that the gods could not bring themselves to commune with men. Murray pictures this age as one marking the beginning of spiritual crisis, of asceticism, of mysticism, of pessimism. "This sense of failure, this progressive loss of hope in the world, in sober calculation, and in organized human effort," he concludes, "threw the later Greek back upon his own soul, upon the pursuit of personal holiness, upon emotions, mysteries and revelations, upon the comparative neglect of this transitory and imperfect world for the sake of some dream-world far off, which shall subsist without sin or corruption, the same yesterday, to-day, and for ever." [47] In such a milieu man could not hope either for heaven or for a new revelation of God. As a result, man, Epicurus believed, must seek to make himself like a god through withdrawal and resignation.

Strange, even paradoxical, as it may sound, Epicurus' religious teachings were in some respects mystical; they contained those elements that Murray refers to, though harshly and unjustly, as the "spiritual exaltation which is so often the companion of morbidity." Dean Inge's definition of mysticism as "the attempt to realise the presence of the living God in the soul and in nature, or, more generally, as *the attempt to realise, in thought and feeling, the immanence of the temporal in the eternal, and of the eternal in the temporal*," [48] can be applied to Epicurus' religious position. For although Epicurus did not embrace the mystical principle of union (*enosis*) with God, he did express the belief that the highest good is the greatest likeness to the gods of the *intermundia*.

In evaluating Epicurus' religious views as a kind of mystical materialism, we must not slight the mystical element. Indeed, his views constitute a qualified mysticism, communicating both an immediacy and a power of feeling. At this point, his religious thought (along with that of Plato, interestingly enough) admits to the realization that man's earthly existence is haunted by the presence of an invisible and eternal world beyond; that, by emulating the *ataraxia* of the gods, man can purge the mind of vices and ultimately attain a transcending happiness; that man can, by his rejection of the outer life, escape and rise above a jarring world. However, escape has its own connotations in Epicurus' religious thought, connotations which serve to clarify the material facets of his mysticism.

Epicurus' escape can best be understood in comparison with Plato's. For Plato, escape from the earthly world meant the pilgrimage of the soul and its ascent to divine union with the source (demiurge) from which all being emerged: "Wherefore we ought to fly away from earth to heaven as quickly as we can;" Plato says, "and to fly away means to become like God, as far as this is possible; and to become like him, means to become holy, just, and wise." [49] Furthermore, according to Plato, the soul, which is divine and immortal, is liberated from the body by death and then makes its way into "the serene air of eternal life" and the world of Ideas, which are outside time and space. Always it is the movement towards God, the activity towards the object of the

vision or the contemplation with which the thinker becomes identified that dominates Plato's teachings.

Epicurus, on the other hand, visualized escape as a part of the
journey of the body in the brief time allotted to it. For him, the
body and, necessarily, the soul were mortal. Thus, escape meant
liberation from the outer world of human activity to a private
domain (the garden) where man could enjoy glad hours of
friendship as well as of contemplation of the gods, who could be
imitated but never joined. Nor, to be sure, could Epicurus tolerate
what Velleius in Cicero's dialogue speaks of as "the artisan deity
and world-builder of Plato's *Timaeus,* or that old hag of a fortune-
teller, the *Pronoia* (which we may render 'Providence') of the
Stoics; nor yet a world endowed with a mind and senses of its
own, a spherical, rotatory god of burning fire; these are the mar-
vels and monstrosities of philosophers who do not reason but
dream." [50] If, therefore, Epicurus shared Plato's love of contemplation, it was the contemplation of what could materialize in human
existence and not in an eternal beyond. If he stressed, as did
Plato, the importance of piety, it was an energizing piety that
achieved meaning in a community of believers and in the essential
present, not in some noetic experience and state of ecstasy.

As one might expect, Epicurus' deviations from religious ortho-
doxy and his pleas for enlightenment and reform met with great
opposition. A religious nonconformist, he was abused as a heretic
and as an atheist. Plutarch, for example, in his polemic against the
Epicurean Colotes, speaks of the followers of Epicurus who "go
not round about the bush, as they say, not secretly and by circuit
of covert speeches, but openly and even at the first assault set upon
the principal point of all, to wit, the opinion of God and Religion." [51] In Cicero's *On the Nature of the Gods,* Cotta, who posits
the Academic position in theology and presents the charges of
atheism against Epicurus, concludes his discussion with the contention that by abolishing divine beneficence and benevolence,
the Greek philosopher "uprooted and exterminated all religion
from the human heart." [52]

XI *"Alexander the False Prophet"*

A more violent but not less unusual indictment of Epicurus as
an atheist was that of the false priest of Asclepius, Alexander of
Abonoteichus in Asia Minor. His activity, covering the years

150–170 after Christ, is described in an account entitled "Alexander the False Prophet" by Lucian, a Greek satirist and prose writer (*ca.* A. D. 120–200). Lucian's account brings out by way of contrast the sincerity and the power of Epicurus' religious thought as opposed to the religious hypocrisy personified by Alexander, whose cult made headway not only in Asia Minor, extending over Pontus, Ionia, Cilicia, Paphlagonia, and Galatia, but also in other parts of the Roman world.

Centering his new religion on a sacred snake and making claims to divine origin, Alexander "made predictions and gave oracles, employing great shrewdness in it and combining guess work with his trickery." His oracles were anxiously received and very expensively paid for by beguiled persons, "thick-witted, uneducated fellows that they were"! That he received as much as seventy or eighty thousand drachmas a year for delivering oracles was not remarkable—"since men were so greedy as to send in ten and fifteen questions each." Obviously he needed a great deal of money: he had built up a big religious organization, and around him there had now gathered "assistants, servants, collectors of information, writers of oracles, custodians of oracles, clerks, sealers, and expounders." He even had his own missionaries who went abroad to publish his fame and "to say that he made predictions, discovered fugitive slaves, detected thieves and robbers, caused treasures to be dug up, healed the sick, and in some cases had actually raised the dead." Alexander could not keep all the treasure for himself, but "divided with all, giving each one what was proportionate to his worth." [53]

Alexander's trickery, however, did not go undetected. Followers of Epicurus, joined by Christians, protested against him, and he in turn issued a promulgation that "Pontus was full of atheists and Christians who had the hardihood to utter the vilest abuse of him." It is not at all surprising that he detested Epicurus. "Upon whom else," Lucian asks, "would a quack who loved humbug and bitterly hated truth more fittingly make war than upon Epicurus, who discerned the nature of things and alone knew the truth in them?" Thus, Alexander termed the Greek philosopher "the impervious Epicurus," against whom he delivered an oracle which pictured him in Hades: "With leaden fetters on his feet in filthy mire he sitteth." [54] But Alexander was not content with a mere oracle. Religious nonconformity must be expunged; Epicurus' writings must be proscribed.

The persecution of nonconformists has always plagued human history. They must inevitably suffer for their independent spirit of inquiry and for their protests of conscience. Often, if a nonconformist is not himself jailed or burned at the stake, his writings are attacked and banned. Those, too, who embrace his opinions are often harried and threatened. Alexander the False Prophet adopted typically totalitarian methods in opposing the efforts of the Epicureans of his time to unmask him. Thus, he called them atheists and ridiculed them as "Epicureans," a word which early in history acquired overtones of denunciation. In particular he focused his attacks on Epicurus' writings, especially the *Principal Doctrines*. Lucian reports that Alexander brought this work "into the middle of the market-place, burned it on fagots of fig-wood just as if he were burning the man in person, and threw the ashes into the sea, even adding an oracle also: 'Burn with fire, I command you, the creed of a purblind dotard.' " [55] Such were the remedies of a false physician!

XII *Religious Nonconformity*

Religious nonconformity, which is not for the weak or the irresolute, may experience long periods of suppression, but it never dies. Doubtless, religious inquisitors like Alexander remained as eternal enemies of Epicurus' thought, the abuse of which continued well after the time of the false prophet. (We can imagine why so few of Epicurus' writings have come down to us.) But although it was reviled, Epicureanism lived on until the fourth century. Then, as the civilized world was breaking down and perishing in blood, Epicureanism fell asleep. "Is it dead?" Bonnard asks. "Do not believe it," he replies; "it can never die; it is one of the authentic faces of mankind. A sleeping face, wrapped in sullen slumber. Go and see it in Rome, at the *Museo delle Terme;* the head of the Sleeping Erinye. It has the face of one who rejects our passing day, yet is ready to wake when these times of enigma bring in the world it dreams of. . . ." [56]

In a famous inscription discovered at Oenoanda, the old Epicurean Diogenes left a message that has survived as a compendium of Epicurean religious thought. His message reflects the greatness and the inspiration of Epicurus' religious teachings. Above all, it is the kind of message which makes nonconformity worth all the struggle which it must undergo in order to foster enlightenment, to cure men of foolish but deadly weaknesses, and to bring about, in William James's words, "the religion of healthy-mindedness":

Now that age has brought me to the sunset of my days, and I expect hourly to have to leave the world lamenting the plentitude of my joy, I have resolved to give some help now, lest I should lack the time later, to those in a right state of mind. If one man, or two, or three or four or as many as you will, called on me for help in distress, I would do all in my power to counsel him well. And today, as I have said, the most part of mankind are sick, as of an epidemic; their sickness is their false beliefs about the world, and it is worsening as it spreads by imitation from one to another, as among a flock of sheep. Moreover it is only right to succour those that will come after us—they also belong to us, though they are not yet born, and love for man bids us help any strangers that may pass this way.[57]

CHAPTER 5

The Soul

EPICURUS' concept of the soul (*psychē*) is best examined in contrast with Homer's concept of the soul as descending into the darkness of the kingdom of the dead, ruled over by the detested Hades and the dreaded Persephone, and with Plato's concept of the soul as finally ascending into the light of the higher realm from which it originated. The Homeric view of death as the "hateful darkness" and the Platonic vision of a "heavenly pilgrimage" were equally distasteful to Epicurus, who repudiated both the fear of nothingness which gripped Homeric man and the religious hope provided by "the golden Plato," as Epicurus sarcastically referred to him. Such attitudes were conducive, respectively, to fatalism (*moira*) and to a vague metaphysics, both of which, Epicurus warned, disturb man's equanimity. When Epicurus discussed the soul, therefore, he spoke neither as a poet nor as a seer, but rather as a healer of pain. His paramount aim was always to overcome the enemies of happiness and tranquillity: to lessen the pain of loss and to push aside the agitating desires for immortality that come with thoughts of the death of the body and the release of the soul. "Death," Epicurus says in the second of his *Principal Doctrines*, "is nothing to us: for that which is dissolved is without sensation; and that which lacks sensation is nothing to us."

I *Homer's View*

Homer, although he sings of heroes and their exploits and of the gladness and strength of life, does not fail to speak of the mystery of what happens to the soul after death. It is the active existence of the living, to be sure, that primarily concerns the blind bard: life for him is at once most precious and most challenging. But, although he glorifies physical feats and makes men giants whose voices echo in the history of the race, he cannot escape the realization that there exists a realm in which "dwell the senseless dead, the phantoms of men outworn." "Rather would I live on ground as the hireling of another," the shade of Achilles tells Odysseus during the latter's descent into Hades, "with a landless man who had no great livelihood, than bear sway among all the dead that be departed." [1] These are bitter words, reflecting not only the cruel fact of death but also the yearning for a life that does not end. A great man's glorious name no doubt lives on, but his body dies and disappears and his soul departs. These are final, irrevocable facts: the mightiest attempts to master them are fruitless, even for poets.

It is as "shades" and "images" that Homer refers to departed souls. How else could he evoke the nothingness of life that has ceased? For with death Homer sees the extinction of all feelings and the departure of the soul into a realm of shadows. At death the soul is relegated to "a land desolate of joy" where "the night is of great length, unspeakable." Now the soul commences its sojourn in "the undiscovered country," in a barren, gloomy region, Erebus, in "the dark house of chill Hades," with its "shadowy halls" and its "deadly night," eternally "shrouded in mist and cloud, and never does the shining sun look down." This twilight land of the dead is pictured by Homer as located far distant from the living cosmos. To reach it the soul must travel "to the limits of the world, to the deep flowing Oceanus." "Between us and you," Odysseus' mother says to him, "are great rivers and dreadful streams; first Oceanus, which can no wise be crossed on foot, but only if one have a well-wrought ship." [2]

Except to Tityos, Tantalos, and Sisyphus, who committed outrageous sins against the Olympian deities, no punishments or rewards are meted out to the inhabitants of Homer's Hades. The shades that come to the underworld are henceforth without past or future, forever the captives of "the powerful warder," of "the unseen one." Insignificant, shadowy, these souls are forever cut off from the living. A certain bleakness and a hopelessness, therefore, are associated with departed souls. "The Homeric picture of the shadow-life of the disembodied soul," Rohde declares, "is the work of resignation, not of hope." [3] Thus, in Homer's view the departed soul personifies loss of vitality, of physical vigor; by the nature of its insubstantiality, it represents an eclipse of life. "The life after death," Nilsson observes in this connection, "has been brought closer to the life on earth but has also lost its power and intensity. Instead of a copy, it has become a pale shadow." [4] More than anything else, perhaps, Homer's abode of shades dramatizes the experience of de-creating and of de-energizing that is inherent in death. The state of the soul now emphasizes the negation of life, as the soul remains immobilized in a remote region, like a gaunt and ageless prisoner, numbed by an aeon of inactivity, totally oblivious of anything around it, sentenced to an everlasting inanition which knows neither rest nor exertion. A dreamless half-sleep beckons within the gates of hell—a cause, to borrow Hadrian's well-known lines, more of "regret for the sunlight left behind than any hope in entering on a dim journey into the unknown."

II *Plato's View*

In Plato's concept of the soul, on the other hand, it is the quality of deathlessness that is emphasized. The philosophical and theological implications of his theories are seen especially in his famous dialogue *Phaedo*. Whereas in Homer it is a poet of the flesh who is speaking, in Plato it is a poet of the spirit and a "priestly man of wisdom." Unlike Homer, who celebrates physical life and laments its demise with imagery of shadows and darkness, Plato affirms that life is preparation for death. His hero is not he who conquers cities or defeats the strongest of the enemy but rather he who studies the meaning of death. For Plato death marks the point at which the soul is no longer "nailed and glued" to the body but is liberated at last from the evils of the body. Death, Plato feels, means "release of the soul from the chains of the body," which have kept it from truth and vision. Death is an occasion for joy, as the soul achieves its longed-for purification, passing at last "into the other world, the region of purity, and eternity, and immortality, and unchangeableness, which are her kindred, and with them she ever lives." [5]

To Plato the existence of the soul explains the existence of the world. Accordingly, the soul is "older than the body." Divine and immortal, it is the source of all life and of all movement. "For the body which is moved from without," Plato reasons in the *Phaedrus*, "is soulless; but that which is moved from within has a soul, for such is the nature of the soul." [6] The souls of heavenly bodies, of men, of animals, and of plants, he thought, are all created by God; and, once created, they can never be destroyed, for such destruction would be inconsistent with the goodness of God. Earthly life constitutes for the soul a brief period of exile, during which it "is infected with the evils of the body," troubled by the requirement of food and drink, liable to diseases which impede the search after "true being," "dragged down" by love, lust, and fear, which result in wars and factions. In effect, the body, with its "lower life of ambition" and its "slavish" pleasures, keeps man from a vision of truth. The "lover of the body" is fearful of death, for he believes that truth exists only in bodily form and that when the soul "has left the body, her place may be nowhere, and that on the very day of death she may perish and come to an end . . . issuing forth dispersed like smoke or air and in her flight vanishing away into nothingness." [7] The "lover of wisdom," on the other hand, knows that pure knowledge lies outside the body; hence, philosophy becomes a "rehearsal of death."

The central task of the soul, then, is to free itself from its impure companion in "the region of the changeable," that is, from the corporeal element which is "heavy and weighty and earthy." "For Plato," as Rohde observes, "the Souls live on as they had been in the beginning—individual beings conscious of themselves in a time that has no end and is beyond all time. He teaches a personal immortality." [8] The proper jewels of the soul, to Plato, are temperance, justice, courage, nobility, and truth, as opposed to the pleasures and ornaments of the body. An independent, ethereal substance that comes from beyond space and time into a perceptible and material world, subject to flux and decay, the soul must struggle with the tendencies of the body and with the illusions of the senses before it finds again the "way upwards" and ultimate salvation in the heaven of the spiritual world of eternal laws and patterns. The soul's soaring to a transcendental world of total blessedness, rest, and security is described by Plato in these words:

That soul . . . herself invisible, departs to the invisible world—to the divine and immortal and rational: thither arriving, she is secure of bliss and is released from the error and folly of men, their fears and wild passions and all other human ills, and forever dwells, as they say of the initiated, in company with the gods.[9]

III   *Epicurus' Concept of the Corporeal Soul*

Epicurus, who was thoroughly familiar with Homer, as all educated Greeks of his time were, and with Plato (through the teachings of Xenocrates in Athens and Pamphilus in Samos, if not
otherwise), diverged from both of them in his concept of the soul.
A staunch materialist who believed that everything must be referred to the tests of the senses and of the feelings, Epicurus spec-
ified that the soul is "a body of fine particles distributed throughout the whole structure." For his concept we must rely on his
Letter to Herodotus and on lines 94–829 of Book III of Lucretius'
On the Nature of Things.

Although Epicurus concurred with the Homeric and the Platonic views that man is composed of both body and soul and that
upon death the soul departs from the body, he insisted at the
same time that the soul is corporeal. "Now it is impossible," he
writes, "to conceive the incorporeal as a separate existence, except
the void: and the void can neither act nor be acted upon, but only
provides opportunity of motion through itself to bodies." [10] Hence,
because the soul can act and be acted upon, it is corporeal. "Now
all this," he notes, "is made manifest by the activities of the soul
and the feelings and the readiness of its movements and its processes of thought and by what we lose at the moment of death." [11]
In more specific terms Lucretius underlines the concrete nature of
the soul: he points out that the soul survives when much of the
body is lost but that with the loss of particles of vital heat and air
it dies.

IV   *Mind and Spirit*

On the basis of Lucretius' discourses, we can more or less assume that Epicurus drew a distinction between the higher or intelligent principle of the soul, mind (*animus; to logikon*), and the
animal, vital principle, spirit (*anima; to alogon*). "Ever bound to
each other," mind and spirit "make up a single nature," that is, the
soul; but the mind is the "directing and governing principle." For
although there is no difference in the material makeup of spirit
and of mind, the latter is the more active. "The mind," as Lucretius defines its task, "has more to do with holding the fastnesses of
life and has more sovereign sway over it. . . . For without the
understanding and the mind no part of the soul can maintain it-

self in the frame the smallest fraction of time. . . ." [12] Its seat is in the middle region of the breast, Lucretius further points out; here "throb fear and apprehension, about these spots dwell soothing joys; therefore here is the understanding or mind. All the rest of the soul disseminated through the whole body obeys and moves at the will and inclination of the mind." [13]

Moreover, the mind can have pain and joy by itself, even when there is nothing to stir either soul or body. But when some strong feeling stirs the mind, "we see the whole soul feel in unison through all the limbs, sweats and paleness spread over the whole body, the tongue falter, the voice die away, a mist cover the eyes, the ears ring, the limbs sink under one." [14] Inevitably, then, the mind acts upon the body by touch when it is seen "to push the limbs, rouse the body from sleep, and alter the countenance and guide and turn about the whole man." [15] Obversely, the sufferings of the body affect the mind, such as when "a weapon with a shud-der-causing force has been driven in and has laid bare bones and sinews within the body," followed by faintness and by collapse to the ground—"and on the ground the turmoil of mind . . . arises, and sometimes a kind of undecided inclination to get up." [16]

V Composition of the Soul

As to the composition of the soul, Epicurus believed that it is made up primarily of breath and of heat, which he considered a material substance. In Lucretius, by the way, we find mention of another element, air, which Epicurus probably included in texts now lost. In this connection Bailey notes that "the three elements were used by Epicureans, as by Lucretius, to explain differences of character and moods of feeling both in human beings and in animals." [17] Epicurus believed that the soul also contains an un-known element "which is many degrees more advanced . . . in fineness of composition, and for this reason is more capable of feeling in harmony with the rest of the structure as well." [18]

Lucretius supplies further details concerning this hidden fourth element: "It is altogether without name; than it nothing exists more nimble or more fine, or of smaller or smoother elements." Above all, this fourth element, which is indeed "the very soul so to say of the whole soul," as well as the seat of will and of thought, causes the soul's sensation. Or as Aetios phrases it: "Of these four elements that of breath gives the power to move, the airy gives tranquillity, the hot produces the perceptible warmth of the body, and the nameless implants the capacity we have for sensation. For in none of the named elements does sensation exist." [19] In the following passage, Lucretius describes how the fourth element transmits sensation:

. . . it first transmits the sense-giving motions through the frame; for it is first stirred, made up as it is of small particles; next the heat and the unseen force of the spirit receive the motions, then the air; then all things are set in action, the blood is stirred, every part of the flesh is filled with sensation; last of all the feeling is transmitted to the bones and marrow, whether it be one of pleasure or an opposite excitement.[20]

Preserving Democritus' belief that the soul is an aggregation of atoms which are small, smooth, and mostly round, forming a "mixture" and not a "texture," Epicurus emphasized that the soul possesses the major cause of sensation. Nevertheless, he also emphasized that it could not have acquired sensation without being enclosed and protected by the whole body. "And this in its turn," writes Epicurus, "having afforded the soul this cause of sensation acquires itself too a share in this contingent capacity from the soul." [21] It is the union of the body and the soul which gives cause to life. "The two adhere together with common roots," Lucretius tells us, "and cannot it is plain be riven asunder without destruction. Even as it is not easy to pluck the perfume out of lumps of frankincense without quite destroying its nature as well; so it is not easy to withdraw from the whole body the nature of the mind and soul without dissolving all alike." [22] Thus, the body is the container of the soul: each is necessary to the other and cannot survive without it. Epicurus further notes that when the soul is released from the body, the body no longer experiences sensation:

For it never possessed this power in itself, but used to afford opportunity for it to another existence, brought into being at the same time with itself: and this existence, owing to the power now consummated within itself as a result of motion, used spontaneously to produce for itself the capacity of sensation and then to communicate it to the body as well, in virtue of its contact and correspondence of movement. . . .[23]

Furthermore, as long as the soul remains in the body, it will never lose sensation, even if some parts of the body are lost. If a portion of the soul is lost with the loss of the part of the body which encloses it, "if the soul continues to exist at all, it will retain sensation." "On the other hand," Epicurus stipulates, "the rest of the structure, though it continues to exist either as a whole or in part, does not retain sensation, if it has once lost that sum of atoms, however small it be, which together goes to produce the nature of the soul." [24] As a result the soul plays a more animate role than the body as a primary cause of sensation and of life itself.

In contrast, the body, which can be conceived of as a receptacle, serves as the proper abode of the soul, and its destruction causes a scattering of the soul and a breakdown of its creative energies. If the body cannot spark the flames of life, it nonetheless provides a necessary protection for them. Its power is not one of creation but of sustenance. In an Aristotelian sense it is an element without whose potentiality the actuality or fulfilment of the soul would not be realized. Of this relationship Epicurus writes:

. . . if the whole structure is dissolved, the soul is dispersed and no longer has the same powers nor performs its movements, so that it does not possess sensation either. For it is impossible to imagine it with sensation, if it is not in this organism and cannot effect these movements, when what encloses and surrounds it is no longer the same as the surroundings in which it now exists and performs these movements.[25]

VI *Lucretius on the Soul's Mortality*

The Epicurean concept of the soul-body relationship and hence of the mortality of the soul comes out fully and graphically in Lucretius' poem, which sets forth multiple proofs of the soul's mortality, "got together by long study and invented with welcome effort." [26] It is believed that Lucretius adapted these proofs from one of the thirty-seven books of Epicurus' *On Nature*. "To link forsooth a mortal thing with an everlasting," Lucretius asserts, "and suppose that they can have sense in common and can be reciprocally acted upon, is sheer folly; for what can be conceived more incongruous, more discordant and inconsistent with itself, than a thing which is mortal, linked with an immortal and everlasting thing, trying in such union to weather furious storms?" Only by combatting the folly of the belief in immortality, and thus of the fear of death, Lucretius tells us, can the Epicurean goal of a happy life be attained.

Lucretius points out that the soul is contained within the body just as water is within a vessel. When the vessel is shattered, the water flows away on all sides; similarly, "the soul too is shed abroad and perishes much more quickly and dissolves sooner into its first bodies, when once it has been taken out of the limbs of a man and has withdrawn." He then goes on to stress that the soul develops with the body and that when "the body has been shattered by the mastering might of time" and all faculties fail, the soul dies. Long before Lucretius and Epicurus, Herodotus described this process: "For along with the body as it grows, the mind also grows; when it ages, the mind also ages and is dulled for all actions." [27]

Continuing, Lucretius argues that just as the body suffers diseases and pain, so does the mind have cares and griefs and fears. Indeed, the diseases of the body ravage the mind. Moreover, the fact that the mind can be healed as a sick body is healed further proves that it has a mortal existence. In amplifying this argument, Lucretius declares that as life gradually dies in the body, so too must the soul gradually perish. Once the soul is driven out of the body, it dissolves; thus the fact is made quite evident that the body is the only proper abode of the soul. "But neither eyes nor nose nor hand," he writes, "can exist for the soul apart from the body nor can tongue, nor can ears perceive by the sense of hearing or exist for the soul by themselves apart from the body."

Lucretius then proceeds to show that bits of the soul survive in severed parts of the body, again as evidence of the interdependence of the body and the soul. He also reminds us that we do not remember anything of another existence, an obvious criticism of the Pythagoreans and the Platonists and their doctrine of recollection. Lucretius contends: "If the power of the mind has been so completely changed, that all remembrance of past things is lost, that methinks differs not widely from death; therefore you must admit that the soul which was before has perished and that which now is has been formed." He reasons that if the soul entered the body from without, it could not be so closely connected with it. In truth, he says, the soul is born within the body and perishes as the body perishes. This argument, summarized in the following passage, can be seen specifically as an attack on the concept of the nature and destiny of the soul held by the adherents of Orphism, a Greek religious movement of the seventh and sixth centuries B.C.:

Wherefore, again and again I say, we must believe souls to be neither without a birth nor exempted from the law of death; for we must not believe that they could have been so completely united with our bodies, if they found their way into them from without, nor, since they are so closely inwoven with them, does it appear that they can get out unharmed and unloose themselves unscathed from all the sinews and bones and joints. . . . Wherefore the nature of the soul is seen to be neither without a birthday nor exempt from death.

Later on Lucretius seeks to undermine the Pythagorean doctrine of reincarnation by his insistence that the soul can develop or decline but cannot change generically:

Again why does untamed fierceness go along with the sullen brood of lions, cunning with foxes and proneness to flight with stags? And to take any other instance of the kind, why are all qualities engendered in the limbs and temper from the very commencement of life, if not because a fixed power of mind derived from its proper seed and breed grows up together with the whole body? If it were immortal and wont to pass into different bodies, living creatures would be of interchangeable dispositions; a dog of Hyrcanian breed would often fly before the attack of an antlered stag, a hawk would cower in mid air as it fled at the approach of a dove, men would be without reason, the savage races of wild beasts would have reason. For the assertion that an immortal soul is altered by a change of body is advanced on a false principle. What is changed is dissolved, and therefore dies: the parts are transposed and quit their former order; therefore they must admit of being dissolved too throughout the frame, in order at last to die one and all together with the body.

All things in life, he brings out, have a fixed environment and set conditions of existence: "a tree cannot exist in the ether, nor clouds in the deep sea nor can fishes live in the fields nor blood exist in woods nor sap in stones." By the same token the soul cannot come into being without the body "nor exist far away from the sinews and blood." Subject always to destructive powers, the soul can never retreat "from death-bringing things" but must ever fall sick with the diseases of the body:

it sickens in sympathy with the maladies of the body, it is often attacked by that which frets it on the score of the future and keeps it on the rack of suspense and wears it out with cares; and when ill deeds are in the past, remorse for sins yet gnaws: then there is madness peculiar to the mind and forgetfulness of all things; then too it often sinks into the black waters of lethargy.

VII *"The Incubus of Superstition"*

The salient feature of the Epicurean approach to the soul is, to be sure, the repudiation of the inherence of a divine element, especially as held by the Platonists. This repudiation was part of Epicurus' reaction to his times. As Murray indicates, the whole tendency of Greek philosophy after Plato was away from the outer world towards the world of the soul.[28] Eventually this world was made visible in the cult of the immortal hero. "To the people who were at all accustomed to the conception of a God-Man," Murray states, "it was difficult not to feel that the conception was realized in Alexander." [29] A nonconformist thinker like Epicurus had to be opposed to the deification of Alexander the Great, "the son of Zeus and Poseidon," whose cult flourished near Teos, for instance, until the days of the Roman Empire, and of his successors such as Seleucus, Ptolemaeus, Antigonus, and Demetrius, who were addressed as "divine saviors" (*theoi sōtēres*). Epicurus wished to offset Hellenistic ecclesiasticism, with its hymns, priesthoods, altars, images, and sacrifices, and to rescue "the human mind from the incubus of superstition." [30] To this end he denied the immortality of the soul. Man, he taught, would be able to overcome fear and to affirm life only by rejecting a belief in human immortality which the Roman Stoic Seneca was to depict as stretching "lame hands" to a "birthday of eternity." [31]

CHAPTER 6

Happiness

WHAT is happiness? To ancient Greek philosophers like Plato, Aristotle, Zeno the Stoic, and Epicurus, this question was of profound importance, and they devoted much thought to it. Taking Greek philosophy as a whole and examining therein the concept of happiness in its broadest ethical contexts, we can say that "Happiness . . . in every Greek system of religion or philosophy, is singleness of aim, uprightness of heart, and the undisturbed peace of one who rests in ultimate truth, and has hold of reality." [1]

In general, the Greek philosophers approached the meaning of happiness on the basis of their estimations of two elements which affect the human condition adversely: disorder (in man and around him) and pain (physical and mental). Hence, to gain victory over the disorderly elements in existence and to endure, to lessen, and if possible to remove pain were needs that the Greek philosophers related directly to man's search for happiness and to his general conduct. Happiness was thought to depend on one's understanding and accepting the world-order. Although the Greek philosophers did not agree on the structure of the world-order or on a definition of happiness, and although they advocated various, even conflicting, modes of conduct directed toward the attainment of happiness, they shared the conviction that it is the desired end of human experience.

I *The Discernment of Pleasure*

Epicurus was unequivocal in his teaching that happiness is the highest good, the beginning and end of which is pleasure. Indeed, he believed that pleasure and pain supply the motives of desire and of avoidance, that is, of all human conduct. It would be a gross injustice to deny the presence in his ethical doctrine of such traditional Hellenic virtues as wisdom, temperance, and courage or strength of soul. What he did was to appraise the values of these virtues in proportion to man's attainment of pleasure and ultimately of happiness. It is within each man's power, he insisted, to achieve happiness by the eradication of pain and by the cultivation of those powers in the physical world and in man himself that produce self-sufficiency (*autarkeia*). For Epicurus, happiness was characterized by the freedom from fear, the absence of pain, and the culmination of "stabilized pleasure," at which point one achieves a perfect tranquillity, or *ataraxia*.

Yet happiness predicates, as will be seen, a delicate and perfect equilibrium resulting from prudent reflection on and discernment of pleasures. In this discernment lies the cardinal virtue: The wise man who possesses this virtue is not necessarily one who is in possession of pleasure but one who is able to proceed rightly in the quest for pleasure. Virtue, then, is the best way to happiness. "It is not possible to live pleasantly," Epicurus insisted, "without living prudently and honourably and justly, nor again to live a life of prudence, honour, and justice without living pleasantly. And the man who does not possess the pleasant life, is not living prudently and honourably and justly, and the man who does not possess the virtuous life, cannot possibly live pleasantly." [2]

In a sense, Epicurus sought not only to re-evaluate but also to readjust, as it were, the whole concept of happiness, so as to achieve a balance between the virtue that helps to sustain men "within the limits of nature" and the need to overcome any traces of a morality which does not produce pleasure. It is precisely this balance which signals the originality of Epicurus' doctrine of happiness and the variety of its aspects, which Robin summarizes in this passage:

[Epicureanism] declares pleasure to be the highest good, and diminishes it by asceticism; it places resignation side by side with beatitude, and melancholy with optimism; its thorough sensualism is supplemented by a reasoned calculation of pleasures; it is materialistic, and seeks its foundation in thought; it is scornful of scientific truth, and bases conduct on the knowledge of nature; into mechanism it introduces liberty; it combats superstition, and preaches a faith.[3]

The realities of human experience, confined between birth and death, served as the only basis of Epicurus' approach not only to happiness but also to the whole of his moral system. Happiness, he maintained, is perceived by the senses and not known by metaphysical abstractions or ideals, nor by a belief in a transcendent beauty of virtues: "The wealth demanded by nature is both limited and easily procured; that demanded by idle imaginings stretches on to infinity." [4] The standard by which we judge every good consists of the physical feelings: "We must consider both the real purpose and all the evidence of direct perception, to which we always refer the conclusions of opinion; otherwise, all will be full of doubt and confusion." [5] Hence, if man fought against all sensations, he would have no standard by which to judge even those which he claims are false.

II *The Truth of Sensation*

Not to refer one's actions to the end of nature brings error, even as the removal of sight, association, and contact brings an end to the passion of love. "I know not how I can conceive the good," Epicurus says, "if I withdraw the pleasures of taste, and withdraw the pleasures of love, and withdraw the pleasures of hearing, and withdraw the pleasurable emotions caused to sight by beautiful form." [6] As Bailey emphasizes, Epicurus "is not concerned with what 'ought' to be or what is 'fitting,' but simply with what is." [7] Nothing can refute a sensation. Even reason cannot deny the truth of sensation, for reason itself depends on sensation. "Well, then," Lucretius notes, "what must fairly be accounted of higher certainty than sense? Shall reason founded on false sense be able to contradict them, wholly founded as it is on the senses? And if they are not true, then all reason as well is rendered false." [8]

Epicurus had no doubts concerning the goals of his moral theory, goals that by their nature and scope were clearly defined as well as completely disconnected from the abstract and the ideal. Underscoring the concreteness of Epicurus' theory, Cicero described it as one that attempts to supply "courage to face the fear of death; resolution to resist the terrors of religion; peace of mind, for it removes all ignorance of the mysteries of nature; self-control, for it explains the nature of the desires and distinguishes their different kinds." [9]

In this respect, above all, Epicurus' thought must be seen as antithetical to Plato's, which held that the highest good is not pleasure or knowledge but the greatest possible likeness to God as the absolutely good. Happiness, as Plato conceived it, is rooted not in the natural world but in a transcendental world of ideal forms and truth and goodness; at the same time, and perhaps even more importantly, this happiness is restricted to a select few. Epicurus, on the other hand, denying any incompatibility between pleasure and virtue, viewed pleasure as the end of life (*telos*) and virtue as the way thereto. Anyone, he stressed, can attain pleasure and happiness. Furthermore, if Plato was preoccupied with the practice of dying, Epicurus was preoccupied with the art of living. "Was he [Epicurus]," asks L. Manlius Torquatus, who expounds Epicurus' ethic in Cicero's dialogue *About the Ends of Goods and Evils,* "to occupy himself like Plato with music and geometry, arithmetic and astronomy, which starting from false premises cannot be true, and which moreover if they were true would contribute nothing to make our lives pleasanter and therefore better? Was he, I say, to study arts like these, and neglect the master art, so difficult and correspondingly so fruitful, the art of living?" [10]

III *Epicurus and Cyrenaicism*

For Epicurus the good life was impossible without pleasure. His theory of pleasure, which looms so large in the whole of his approach to happiness, goes back to the Cyrenaic or Hedonic School, which is believed to have been founded by Aristippus (*ca.* 435–386 B.C.), a pupil of Socrates, at Cyrene. The Cyrenaics, like the Epicureans after them, held that one can know only through the senses and that one should learn to enjoy, for pleasure is the moral good. Above all, the enjoyment of the present is the true business of man, for only the present is in one's power. Such a view was not, however, a rationalization for licentious behavior. Aristippus, it is said, required his disciples to control, and not to be controlled by, their pleasures. "It is not abstinence from pleasures that is best," he declares, "but mastery over them without ever being worsted." [11]

Even on the basis of a brief summary of Cyrenaic beliefs, it is possible to detect why Epicurus was charged with plagiarizing Aristippus' theory of pleasure and teaching it as his own. (Terming him "the Herbert Spencer of antiquity," Santayana asserts that Epicurus was "an encyclopaedia of second-hand knowledge.") [12] Once, however, it is admitted that Epicurus' ethical theory was a derivation in a riper form of the Aristippian doctrine of sense-pleasure, making way for deeper reflection, the charge of plagiarism becomes indefensible.

What especially stands out is that, whereas the Cyrenaics defined pleasure as movement, implying intense, even violent activity, Epicurus believed that the reality of pleasure exists in sensations which are in "a state of rest." Thus, he emphasized pleasure that was neutral and static. Furthermore, the Cyrenaics gave a predominant role to bodily wants, but Epicurus, like Democritus, stressed the greater importance of mental pleasures. Epicurus, according to Diogenes Laertius, differed from the Cyrenaics in that he held "pains of the mind to be the worse; . . . [for] the flesh endures the storms of the present alone, the mind those of the past and future as well as the present." [13] To the Cyrenaics the happy man was the one who responds fully and spontaneously to sensations of any kind; to the Epicureans the happy man was the one who attains a wisdom of discrimination and of reflection that ultimately leads to a blessed existence of painlessness (*aponia*) and quietude. As Strodach observes, "Cyrenaicism was what Epicureanism has always tended to become in the hands of its lay practitioners." [14]

A recognition of these facts should help to clear Epicurus of the charges of sensualism and debauchery that have so often been used against him. Epicurus, it needs to be pointed out, was concerned with the whole of life and not with mere moments of pleasure, with "each moment deemed an eternity." [15] "For most men," Epicurus writes, "rest is stagnation and activity madness." [16] Thus, the Epicureans, though they seek pleasure and equate it with the highest good, realize the importance of tempering the passions and the appetites, as is made clear in random pronouncements like the following:

Infinite time contains no greater pleasure than limited time, if one measures by reason the limits of pleasure. [17]

He who has learned the limits of life knows that that which removes the pain due to want and makes the whole of life complete is easy to obtain; so that there is no need of actions which involve competition. [18]

It is not the stomach that is insatiable, as is generally said, but the false opinion that the stomach needs an unlimited amount to fill it. [19]

[102]

As evidence that pleasure is the end, Epicurus adduced the fact that living things from the time of their birth are content with pleasure but are at enmity with pain. Epicurus' statement that "the beginning and the root of all good is the pleasure of the stomach" [20] must not, however, be accepted at its face value, nor must he be attacked as preaching a reckless hedonism. His central aim was to differentiate between positive desires, which lead to happiness, and negative desires, which lead to pain. A proper regard for these distinctions, he maintained, will result in the right conduct of life. "The stable condition of well-being in the body," he declared, "and the sure hope of its continuance holds the fullest and surest joy for those who can rightly calculate it." [21] He admits, of course, that all pleasures are natural and good, but he demands that one must always weigh the consequences of pleasures and pains.

IV   *Right Calculation*

In his endeavor to destroy the argument that all kinds of pleasure are to be pursued, Epicurus gave special attention to right calculation. "For it is not continuous drinkings and revellings," he writes to Menoeceus, "nor the satisfaction of lusts, nor the enjoyment of fish and other luxuries of the wealthy table, which produce a pleasant life, but sober reasoning, searching out the motives for all choice and avoidance, and banishing mere opinions, to which are due the greatest disturbances of the spirit." The reasoning powers of the mind, above all, play an important role in giving harmony and refinement to pleasures:

The flesh perceives the limits of pleasure as unlimited and unlimited time is required to supply it. But the mind, having attained a reasoned understanding of the ultimate good of the flesh and its limits and having dissipated the fears concerning the time to come, supplies us with the complete life, and we have no further need of infinite time: but neither does the mind shun pleasure, nor, when circumstances begin to bring about the departure from life, does it approach its end as though it fell short in any way of the best life.[22]

Epicurus' philosophy has been termed not as a teaching per se but as "an activity, which by reasons and reflections procures the happy life." [23] It is precisely "reasons and reflections" that, as seen, distinguish Epicurus' moral theory from that of the Cyrenaics. His wise man, thus, always adheres to the principle of selection; that is, "he rejects pleasures to secure other greater pleasures, or else he endures pains to avoid worse pains." [24] In line with this principle, Epicurus separates desires relating to the welfare of the body and the mind into three classes: In the first class he places those desires which are "natural and necessary" for the relief of pain, such as drink for the thirsty. In the second are desires which are "natural but not necessary" for the variety of pleasure, although not needed for removing pain, such as extravagance in food. In the third are desires which are "neither natural nor necessary," such as honors and fame. A "right understanding" of these categories, Epicurus remarks in his *Letter to Menoeceus,* enables one "to refer all choice and avoidance to the health of the body and the soul's freedom from disturbance, since this is the aim of the life of blessedness."

Once the chief goal of avoiding pain and fear is achieved, Epicurus informs Menoeceus, "all the tempest of the soul is dispersed, since the living creature has not to wander as though in search of something that is missing, and to look for some other thing by which he can fulfil the good of the soul and the good of the body." "For it is then," he continues, "that we have need of pleasure, when we feel pain owing to the absence of pleasure; but when we do not feel pain, we no longer need pleasure."

If pleasure constituted for Epicurus the good life (the *dux vitae, dia voluptas,* "divine pleasure the guide of life," as Lucretius phrases it), then pain embodied evil. "The limit of quantity in pleasures," Epicurus observes, "is the removal of all that is painful. Wherever pleasure is present, as long as it is there, there is neither pain of body nor of mind, nor of both at once." [25] Concerning bodily suffering, Epicurus says it is negligible, "for that which causes acute pain has short duration, and that which endures long in the flesh causes but mild pain." [26] He believed that the occurrence of certain bodily pains helps one in guarding against others like them; that it is better to endure some pains "so that we may enjoy greater joys." "Every pleasure then because of its natural kinship to us," he further states, "is good, yet not every pleasure is to be chosen: even as every pain also is an evil, yet not all are always of a nature to be avoided. Yet by a scale of comparison and by the consideration of advantages and disadvantages we must form our judgment on all these matters. For the good on certain occasions we treat as bad, and conversely the bad as good." [27]

V *Physical Pleasure*

Perhaps the most misinterpreted facet of Epicurus' concept of pleasure is that relating to the flesh. In his approach to the satisfaction of physical desire, Epicurus invariably counseled restraint. With the long-term effects of man's choices always in mind, he did not fail to point out the limits of nature. "We must not violate nature," Epicurus affirms, "but obey her; and we shall obey her if we fulfil the necessary desires and also the physical, if they bring no harm to us, but sternly reject the harmful." [28] It needs to be stressed, furthermore, that Epicurus distrusted sexual pleasures, for he felt that at times the means for satisfying some pleasures brought disturbances which in the long run are greater than the immediate satisfaction. Epicurus' treatment of sex was inevitably informed not only by reticence and by the asceticism in his own life but also by his uncompromising belief that sexual love, either heterosexual or homosexual, constitutes a threat to one's equanimity. "Sexual intercourse," he insists, "has never done a man good, and he is lucky if it has not harmed him." [29]

Aphorisms like the following bring out Epicurus' stress on the need for self-control in all physical pleasures:

Unhappiness comes either through fear or through vain and unbridled desire: but if a man curbs these, he can win for himself the blessedness of understanding.[30]

Frugality too has a limit, and the man who disregards it is in like case with him who errs through excess.[31]

Nothing is sufficient for him to whom what is sufficient seems little.[32]

The ungrateful greed of the soul makes the creature everlastingly desire varieties of dainty food.[33]

Again and again, then, Epicurus referred to the need for contentment with a little. The greatest happiness does not come from the wanton enjoyment of physical pleasures but from a life that is free from anxiety. It is the moderation of desires (not their extirpation, as the Stoics believed) and the ability to live simply that provide the true scope of pleasure:

And so plain savours bring us a pleasure equal to a luxurious diet, when all the pain due to want is removed; and bread and water produce the highest pleasure, when one who needs them puts them to his lips. To grow accustomed therefore to simple and not luxurious diet gives us health to the full, and makes a man alert for the needful employments of life, and when after long intervals we approach luxuries disposes us better towards them, and fits us to be fearless of fortune.[34]

Happiness, as Epicurus approached it, is both interrelated with and interdependent upon the health of the body and the health of the soul. He refused, as Cicero points out, to consider any education worth the name that does not school us in this happiness ("nullam eruditionem esse duxit nisi quae beatae vitae disciplinam iuvaret").[35] "Vain is the word of a philosopher," we hear Epicurus saying, "which does not heal any suffering of man. For just as there is no profit in medicine if it does not expel the diseases of the body, so there is no profit in philosophy either, if it does not expel the suffering of the mind." [36]

Epicurus' garden, it can be said, contained the happiness—the calm that Epicurus compared to the expanse of the sea (galēnismos)—which could not be found in the world outside, in the Athens of Hellenistic times. In the garden the seeker became a finder in company with others who sought to triumph over pain and fear. Here one who was no longer bound by the laws of a decaying civilization sought for the balm of Epicurus' spiritual healing: to meditate, to live simply, to live unknown, to achieve finally a blessed state when one becomes "the equal of the gods" and "vies with Zeus himself." This blessed state, Epicurus notes, "belongs not to abundance of riches or dignity of position or any office or power, but to freedom from pain and moderation in feelings and an attitude of mind which imposes the limits ordained by nature." [37] At the beginning of Book II of *On the Nature of Things*, Lucretius provides an unforgettable picture of Epicurus' wise man who has been freed at last from the distresses of life, who no longer wears himself out to no purpose or sweats drops of blood "along the strait road of ambition":

It is sweet, when on the great sea the winds trouble its waters, to behold from land another's deep distress; not that it is a pleasure and delight that any should be afflicted, but because it is sweet to see from what evils you are yourself exempt. It is sweet also to look upon the mighty struggles of war arrayed along the plains without sharing yourself in the danger. But nothing is more welcome than to hold the lofty and serene positions well fortified by the learning of the wise, from which you may look down upon others and see them wandering all abroad and going astray in their search for the path of life, see the contest among them of intellect, the rivalry of birth, the striving night and day with surpassing effort to struggle up to the summit of power and be masters of the world. O miserable minds of men! O blinded breasts! in what darkness of life and in how great dangers is passed this term of life whatever its duration! not to choose to see that nature craves for herself no more than this, that pain hold aloof from the body, and she in mind enjoy a feeling of pleasure exempt from care and fear? Therefore we see that for the body's nature few things are needed at all, such and such only as take away pain.[38]

VI *The Wise Man*

For Epicurus a man who is "most free from trouble" and from anything "that is associated with causes of unlimited desire" has achieved not only tranquillity but also self-sufficiency. One who does not secure these goals cannot make any claim to happiness. Epicurus' wise man will not marry and rear a family, because such actions inevitably impose too many checks and make him a captive of external powers. He chooses to satisfy those desires that lead to imperturbability. He renounces the outer world only to save his inner being. "The most unalloyed source of protection from men," Epicurus states, "which is secured to some extent by a certain force of expulsion, is in fact the immunity which results from a quiet life and the retirement from the world." [39] The wise man's way of life is marked by simple living, by freedom from anxiety and tensions, by an unruffled independence. He has, in effect, gained control over the things of the world that cause fear and pain. "The man who has best ordered the element of disquiet arising from external circumstances," Epicurus writes, "has made those things that he could akin to himself and the rest at least not alien: but with all to which he could not do even this, he has refrained from mixing, and has expelled from his life all which it was of advantage to treat thus." [40]

Ultimately Epicurus' wise man achieves a repose that, as Hicks has observed, can be compared with the Nirvana of the Buddhists.[41] Indeed, according to Epicurus, "even on the rack the wise man is happy." [42] He is so because he is in need of nothing which he cannot find himself. To a large extent he lives in a privileged sanctuary where, with friends who are like himself, he insures an existence that will not be violated by hostile outsiders. Indeed, "laws exist for the sake of the wise, not that they may not do wrong, but that they may not suffer it." [43] In this connection, too, Epicurus insisted that law was made for man, not man for law. "Justice," he writes, "never is anything in itself, but in the dealings of men with one another in any place whatever and at any time it is a kind of compact not to harm or be harmed." [44]

Always, too, the wise man is able to preserve a delicate balance between commitment to a friend, for whom he will even die if necessary, and the quiet joys of solitude. "As many as possess the power to procure complete immunity from their neighbours," reads the last of the *Principal Doctrines*, "these also live most pleasantly with one another, since they have the most certain pledge of security." [45] But above all, the wise man finds his greatest strength through the recognition of the fact that, though necessity is an evil, "there is no necessity to live under the control of necessity." [46] The source of his strength is also indicated by his ability to dispossess himself of worldly objects that would in any way threaten his peace of mind and body. "A free life," Epicurus teaches, "cannot acquire many possessions, because this is not easy to do without servility to mobs or monarchs, yet it possesses all things in unfailing abundance; and if by chance it obtains many possessions, it is easy to distribute them so as to win the gratitude of neighbours." [47]

There is something saintly about the Epicurean wise man's asceticism, even though this asceticism has as its aim the attainment of peace and self-sufficiency that are of this life. When a certain pain is to be borne, it is borne so that one may avoid fear or greater pain. "It is better for you to be free of fear lying upon a pallet," Epicurus writes, "than to have a golden couch and rich table and be full of trouble." [48] Moreover, when the wise man disciplines his body or rebukes his desires, his actions are not for the purpose of mortifying the flesh, but rather for that of strengthening his self-sufficiency. Indeed, when "he has accommodated himself to straits [the wise man] knows better how to give than to receive: so great is the treasure of self-sufficiency which he has discovered." [49] The Epicurean is a strong man, but not an arrogant or a cruel man. If he has found salvation in his self-sufficiency, he has not forgotten the plight of others who are unhappy. Seneca even claims that "sadness" is at the bottom of the Epicurean way of life and that by its side are "holiness and righteousness."

VII *The Inner Life and the Refining Influences*

It has been remarked that Epicurus' philosophy constitutes a system of selfish, egoistic hedonism: "The wisdom of life of the Epicureans was aesthetic self-enjoyment. Their egoism became delicate and refined, but nevertheless it was still egoism." [50] The validity of this criticism is not to be denied when one carefully views Epicurus' cloistered nonconformity, with its emphasis on withdrawing from the world, on avoiding contact with mass taste, on despising the crude and vulgar aspects of living. Unquestionably, the Epicureans sought for higher refinements and better taste, and they sought to defend the sensitive and to provide for what Zeller speaks of as "dietetics of the soul." [51] By no means was the Epicurean way of life rugged and muscular (athletic contests were disdained, for example), and the competitive spirit was spurned. "It is the health of the valetudinarian," Masson reminds us, "more than of the athlete which Epicurus has in mind." [52] Still, it would be unfair to picture Epicurus and his followers as victims of ennui. Gentle and genteel traits, after all, are never popular in militant times; especially were they not in the Hellenistic Age. "We must remember," Festugière warns, "that the city, which previously had stood as the ideal to be followed, had perished, and the individual had nothing to look for now but his own contentment." [53]

The solitary, reflective man is able to understand the human condition with an acuteness that is often denied to the man of action. In the quiet of his garden a serene and complete Epicurus ministered to his disciples with a readiness of sympathy. Apart from the world, yet always aware of it, Epicurus, as Lucretius writes, "cleansed men's breasts with truth-telling precepts and fixed a limit to lust and fear and explained what was the chief good which we all strive to reach." [54] His teachings were characterized by the constant desire to protect and preserve both the inner life and the refining influences. It was a desire that is peculiar to gentle heroes like Epicurus who, in Emerson's phrase, struggle to "convert the Furies into Muses, and the hells into benefit."

CHAPTER 7

Friendship

THE yearning for friendship, like the yearning for happiness, is constant in human experience. A man counts it a great joy, says Menander, "if he but have the shadow of a friend." [1] A modern writer defines friendship as "the real implicit reliance of one man on another: as sacred a unison as marriage: only it must be deeper, more ultimate than emotion and personality, cool separateness and yet the ultimate reliance." [2] With almost monotonous repetition, "essayers upon friendship" (to quote Joseph Addison's apt phrase) remind us that friendship complements love, lessens pain, warms the heart, sustains the intelligence, inspires the imagination, overcomes loneliness, redoubles joys, and cuts griefs in half. "For there is no man," writes Francis Bacon in his essay "Of Friendship," "that imparteth his joys to his friend, but that he joyeth the more; and no man that imparteth his griefs to his friend, but he grieveth the less." Friendship, then, not only fulfils life but also alleviates the burden of mortality.

Perhaps in no other civilization has friendship been treated with more reverence or with more passion than in ancient Greece. "Friendship goes dancing round the world proclaiming to us all to awake to the praises of a happy life." [3] Thus did Epicurus sing of it. With the possible exception of David's lament for Jonathan in the Old Testament, no other words in literature have better caught the spirit of or entered into the sacred boundaries and sentiments of friendship.

Because of the small population in ancient Greece, the making of friendships was greatly facilitated. Furthermore, because of the subordinate, though by no means unworthy, position of women, the place of friendship among men was accorded a recognition which in the modern world is usually accorded to the place of marriage and the family. Although Greek life was by no means misogynistic, it nevertheless strictly defined the roles of husband

and wife. Even the laws of nature, according to Xenophon, ordained

that each severally should regard the business that is appointed for them. From whence it appears, that it is more convenient for a woman to be at home and mind her domestic affairs, than to gad abroad; and it is as shameful for a man to be at home idling, when his business requires him to be abroad: if any man acts in a different capacity from that he is born to, he breaks through the decrees of Nature, and will certainly meet his punishment, either because he neglects the business which is appointed for him, or because he invades the property of another.[4]

The subordinate status of women is indicated, too, by Pericles' instruction that one should maintain "silence regarding women, silence about their virtues, silence about their misfortune."

The large number of famous friendships in Greek legend and history (*e.g.*, Achilles and Patroclus, Ajax and Teucer, Orestes and Pylades, Harmodius and Aristogeiton, Socrates and Alcibiades, Epaminondas and Pelopidas) attests to the importance of friendship among Greek males. To the ancient Greeks friendship was more than just a fable, a longing, or a dream: it was the subject not only of literature but also of philosophy. No period of ancient Greek history was without its celebration of the golden hours of friendship. We need only turn to some lines of the elegiac and gnomic poet Theognis, who lived in the sixth century B.C., to measure the affection, the devotion, and the tenderness inherent in friendship from early in Greek history. In the following poem Theognis addresses himself to Kurnus, a young nobleman and an intimate of the poet:

> Lo, I have given thee wings wherewith to fly
>   Over the boundless ocean and the earth;
> Yea, on the lips of many shalt thou lie,
>   The comrade of their banquet and their mirth.
> Youths, in their loveliness shall bid thee sound
>   Upon the silver flute's melodious breath;
> And when thou goest darkling underground
>   Down to the lamentable house of death,
> Oh yet not then from honour shalt thou cease
>   But wander, an imperishable name,

Kurnus, about the seas and shores of Greece,
Crossing from isle to isle the barren main.[5]

The Greek word for friendship, *philia*, derives from the verb *philō*, to love; and to the ancient Greeks love and friendship were interdependent. What, then, characterized their concept of friendship was its intimacy, its openness, and its intensity. The kind of cynicism which the eighteenth-century German philosopher Immanuel Kant displayed in his dismissal of the ideal of "emotional friendship" as "the hobby horse of those who write romances" was alien to the ancient Greeks. Among them friendship wore no mask but was glorified as a generous passion which prompted "high thought and heroic action." Far from being a mere romantic ideal, it was an aspect of human experience that reached its highest point in the relation of man to man. Hallowed by philosophers, ennobled by poets, Greek friendship was an organic force of life. When Aristotle in his *Nicomachean Ethics* says that friendship is among man's indispensable requirements, not only as an end but as a means to life,[6] he underscores the virtues of a force which in ancient Greek society played a vital part in the unceasing tension between love and strife.

It has been asserted that the words which the ancient Greeks spoke on the subject of friendship "are not only the most original, but the best."[7] Certainly, the Greek philosophers saw friendship as an elevating and purifying influence, a motivating power of moral life found neither in religion nor in the domestic ties. In this connection a famous scholar has observed, "The history of the Greek schools of philosophy is at the same time the history of friendship."[8] Even a cursory examination of the institution of friendship in ancient Greek life, particularly in the philosophic schools of Pythagoras, of Plato, of Aristotle, and of Epicurus, confirms this statement.

I *Pythagoras and Plato*

In the second half of the sixth century B.C. the Pythagoreans, who mark a good starting point in a discussion of friendship as systematically treated by the philosophers of the ancient world, made up an ascetic brotherhood living in Italy. This brotherhood, which was both a religious order and a school of science, was founded by Pythagoras (*ca.* 582–500 B.C.). Like Epicurus, he was born on the island of Samos; he fled eventually to Croton in southern Italy, apparently to escape the tyranny of Polycrates. The main purpose of the Pythagorean Society was the cultivation of holiness. Hence, Pythagoras advised his disciples

To deem nothing their own. To support the law, to wage war on lawlessness. Never to kill or injure trees that are not wild, nor even any animal that does not injure man. . . . neither to give way to unbridled laughter nor to wear sullen looks. To avoid excess of flesh, on a journey to let exertion and slackening alternate, to train the memory, in wrath to restrain hand and tongue, to respect all divination, to sing to the lyre, and by hymns to show due gratitude to gods and to good men.[9]

Pythagoras, who himself had a great gift for friendship, believed that all men should "behave one to another as not to make friends into enemies, but to turn enemies into friends." [10] The tie of friendship among the Pythagoreans was always strong and revered: they even held that a friend constitutes the half of one's soul. "The love of friends is just concord and equality," [11] the Pythagoreans maintained. The most famous saying of Pythagoras, "Friends have all things in common," best sums up the meaning of friendship in this philosophic school.

The significance that Plato attached to friendship is seen in three of his dialogues, the *Lysis,* the *Symposium,* and the *Phaedrus.* However, his approach to friendship, though eloquent and charming, is not always clear-cut but often clouded by parable, myth, and irony. Plato believed that friendship is a reciprocal relationship possible only between the good, and that high moral character is necessary before the fruition of friendship. What distinguishes Plato's concept, above all, is his belief that friendship serves as an intermediary and as a means toward the achievement of wisdom, beauty, and excellence. In Plato's Academy, therefore, *philia,* like *eros,* was related ultimately to the "contemplation of beauty absolute . . . pure and clear and unalloyed, not clogged with the pollutions of mortality, and all the colours and vanities of human life." For Plato the love felt by one man for another might begin with passion but must gradually lead to a spiritual ideal and vision. Friendship, thus, is by no means an end but rather a means of inspiration in a human relationship that, stage by stage, is metamorphosed into the highest aspiration immortalized in the following passage from the *Symposium:*

He who . . . under the influence of true love, begins to perceive that beauty, is not far from the end. And the true order of going, or being led by another, to the things of love, is to begin from the beauties of earth and mount upwards for the sake of that other beauty, using these as steps only, and from one going on to two, and from two [going on] to all fair forms, and from fair forms to fair practices, and from fair practices to fair notions, until from fair notions he arrives at the notion of absolute beauty, and at last knows what the essence of beauty is.[13]

II *Aristotle*

When we turn to Aristotle's view of friendship, as delineated in Books VIII and IX of the *Nicomachean Ethics,* we attain an understanding of friendship which avoids the ambiguities and the agonizing subtleties of Plato. In a very deep sense Aristotle restored to friendship its most human and humane attributes, and his writings reveal a heartfelt recognition of the gifts of friendship. (At the same time we are able to see "the characteristic Peripatetic blend of an exalted intellectualism with a down-to-earth good sense.")[14] The opening paragraph of Book VIII not only strikes the keynote of Aristotle's treatment of friendship but also manifests the sincerity of his total approach to friendship and its place in human affairs:

For without friends no one would choose to live, though he had all other goods; even rich men and those in possession of office and of dominating power are thought to need friends most of all; for what is the use of such prosperity without the opportunity of beneficence, which is exercised chiefly and in its most laudable form towards friends? Or how can prosperity be guarded and preserved without friends? The greater it is, the more exposed is it to risk. And in poverty and in other misfortunes men think friends are the only refuge. It helps the young, too, to keep from error; it aids older people by ministering to their needs and supplementing the activities that are failing from weakness; those in the prime of life it stimulates to noble actions—"two going together"—for with friends men are more able both to think and to act. Again, parent seems by nature to feel it for offspring and offspring for parent, not only among men but among birds and among most animals; it is felt mutually by members of the same race, and especially by men, whence we praise lovers of their fellowmen. We

[114]

may see even in our travels how near and dear every man is to every other. Friendship seems too to hold states together, and lawgivers to care more for it than for justice; for unanimity seems to be something like friendship, and this they aim at most of all, and expel faction as their worst enemy; and when men are friends they have no need of justice, while when they are just they need friendship as well, and the truest form of justice is thought to be a friendly quality.

Friendship, Aristotle maintained, is noble as well as necessary. He went on to show that there are three kinds of friendship: those based on utility, on pleasure, and on virtue. Perfect friendship, he noted, is the friendship between men who are good ("a virtuous friend seems to be naturally desirable for a virtuous man").[15] Friendship based on virtue is the highest form and the most permanent, though such friendship is the least frequent. Good men are friends for friendship's sake, in virtue of their goodness; they are "friends without qualification," [16] whereas friends for the sake of transient pleasures or selfish utility and advantage are friends incidentally. Loving, rather than being loved, also distinguishes perfect friendship. The wish to be loved, on the other hand, arises out of ambition and is tantamount to a love of flattery. Friendship of the highest kind is restricted to those who are good; friendship based on utility or on pleasure is found in the good, the bad, and the indifferent, and, like the love between children, it disappears as soon as one friend can no longer be of benefit to the other. Aristotle clearly showed that those who are friends on the grounds of virtue are always anxious to do well by each other. Even when one excels the other in the services he renders, there are neither complaints nor quarrels, "for each man desires what is good." At the same time he indicated that a happy man needs friends in all circumstances, for he is essentially "a political creature and one whose nature is to live with others."

As to the number of friends that a person may have, Aristotle advises that "friends in excess of those who are sufficient for our own life are superfluous, and hindrances to the noble life." Precisely because "love is ideally a sort of excess of friendship," great friendships must be confined to only a few people. (Plutarch, echoing this same argument in his essay "On Having Many Friends," claims that "the craving for numerous friends . . . [is] like that of licentious women.")[17] Finally, he likened friendship to a partnership of good men who become better by their activities, who improve each other, and who take from each other "the mould of the characteristics they approve—whence the saying 'noble deeds from noble men.'"

III *Epicurus*

Yet it was Epicurus, "in a single house and that a small one," [18] to quote Cicero, who vivified the noble sentiments and consummated the high hopes in the concepts of friendship advanced by earlier philosophers. In Epicurus' life and teachings, philosophical precepts became living examples, for life in Epicurus' school was a daily exercise in friendship. Epicurus valued friendship so highly that he said that the "noble man" concerns himself chiefly with wisdom and with friendship: "of these, the former is a mortal good, the latter an immortal one." [19] Unlike Pythagoras, he believed that the equal sharing of all things "implied mistrust, and without confidence there is no friendship";[20] unlike Plato, he did not envisage friendship as a step in the education of a future ruler whose goal was the curing of the ills of the body politic; and unlike Aristotle, he did not glorify friendship as a practical activity and as a handmaiden of one's position in the dynamics of social living.

Epicurus' concept of friendship is found in his *Principal Doctrines*, in *The Vatican Sayings*, and in scattered fragments from some of his books and letters. Fragments from the works of Philodemus and parts of Cicero's famous treatise on the theory of ethics, *About the Ends of Goods and Evils*, provide additional sources of information concerning it. Of interest, too, is the fact that Cicero wrote a charming dialogue, *About Friendship*, or *Laelius*, which drew heavily on a famous work on friendship, now lost, by Theophrastus, Aristotle's pupil and successor.

It is evident that the Epicureans made a cult of friendship, bringing together in mystic communion "men and women, rich and poor, old and young, of all nationality and any class." [21] In particular, by welcoming women to his school and by seeing them as potential friends, Epicurus made a revolutionary contribution to the Greek way. Indeed, the presence of women like Themista, Leontion, Mammarion, Hedia, Erotion, and Nikidion in the garden was an unorthodox departure from the predominantly masculine makeup of ancient Greek life.

Naturally, Epicurus' enlightened view of women and the importance that he attached to their position, whether as companions or as wives, evoked severe criticism from his enemies. In the school of Epicurus, Cicero reports, there was never any mention of Lycurgus, Solon, Miltiades, Themistocles, and Epaminondas, "who are always on the lips of the other philosophers." Yet, he asks, "Would it not be better to talk of these than to devote those bulky volumes to Themista?" [22] Nevertheless, it is evident that in Epicurus' school the relations between men and women, far from being either frivolous or scandalous, as some critics foolishly charged (or imagined), gave to women a respect and a dignity that not only made them the equals of men but also showed that they have more to contribute to life than just bearing children and rearing families.

IV *The Values of Friendship*

"Every man," Epicurus says, "passes out of life as if he had just been born." [23] Nevertheless, he believed that a good life can be free from pain and fear, for "wherever pleasure is present and as long as it continues, there is neither suffering nor grieving nor both together." [24] In this respect Epicurus imagined life as a journey of adventure and of discovery:

While we are on the journey of life, we must try to make what is before us better than what is past; but when we come to the journey's end, we must be content and calm. [25]

In the course of this journey and in pursuit of the pleasure, the contentment, and the calm of which he speaks, Epicurus believed that friendship fills one of man's greatest needs:

Of the things that wisdom prepares for insuring lifelong happiness, by far the greatest is the possession of friends. [26]

We must not approve either those who are always ready for friendship, or those who hang back, but for friendship's sake we must even run risks. [27]

Furthermore, he emphasized that the possession of friendship is a security and an immortal blessing:

The same wisdom that permits us to be confident that no evil is eternal or even of long duration also recognizes that in our limited state the security that can be most perfectly gained is that of friendship.[28]

Undoubtedly Epicurus based his concept of friendship on the belief that its motive arises out of self-interest: "Every friendship in itself is to be desired; but the first cause of friendship was a man's needs." [29] He felt that friendship strengthens one's sense of security, especially in times of emergency: "We do not so much need the help of our friends as the confidence of their help in need." [30] Still, one cannot be a true friend who always seeks to exploit another; neither can one be a friend who cannot be depended on for help. If, according to Epicurus, friendship is first prompted by utilitarian motives, it can transcend the egocentric and become something higher once intimacy has developed. Then "the wise man is not more pained when being tortured himself, than when seeing his friend tortured." [31] Then, too, friendship is governed by the realization that it is better to give than to receive. "To love money unjustly gained," he writes, "is evil, and to love money justly gained is shameful; for sordid niggardliness is unseemly even when accompanied by justice." [32]

V *Epicurus and His Disciples*

For Epicurus the word friendship denoted the ultimate relation between mortals. "Nor did he only commend this doctrine by his eloquence," Cicero states, "but far more by the example of his life and conduct." [33] As his several visits to Lampsacus illustrate, Epicurus never forgot his friends. His work radiates with the warmth and the affection that he had for them. "I will sit down and wait for your lovely and godlike appearance," [34] we find him writing to one of his young disciples, Pythocles. His receipt of a letter from another disciple draws this response: "Lord and Saviour, my dearest Leontion, what a hurrahing you drew from us, when we read aloud your dear letter." [35] The absence of friends from his side causes him to exclaim: "If you two don't come to me, I am capable of arriving with a hop, skip, and jump, wherever you and Themista summon me." [36] His concern for the welfare of others was constant, as this fragment from a letter shows: "As I said to you when you were going away, take care also of his brother

Apollodorus. He is not a bad boy, but causes me anxiety, when he does what he does not mean to do." [37]

Although Epicurus was the head of his school, his relation to his followers was always that of a close friend rather than of an authority. He looked on himself as a mentor whose main goal was to teach his followers the art of living wisely and well. Above all, he believed that it is a philosopher's first duty to heal suffering. To the young, in particular, Epicurus' teachings made great appeal, and many chose to become his fervent adherents. The affection they gave him and the genuineness of his response (which recall his dictum that "The veneration of the wise man is a great blessing to those who venerate him")[38] are touchingly depicted in these words addressed to a favorite disciple, Colotes:

In your feeling of reverence for what I was then saying you were seized with an unaccountable desire to embrace me and clasp my knees and show me all the signs of homage paid by men in prayers and supplications to others; so you made me return all these proofs of veneration and respect to you.[39]

VI *Sexual Love*

A primary characteristic of Epicurus' relation to his friends and disciples was his compassionate understanding of the pain which afflicts human life. This characteristic distinguished Epicurus' views on sexual love and his admonitions to his youthful followers. His views on sex were consistently prudent. "No pleasure," he advises, "is a bad thing in itself: but the means which produce some pleasures bring with them disturbances many times greater than the pleasures." [40] Sexual love, he believed, is conducive to these disturbances; for even

When once the pain caused by need has been removed, bodily pleasure will not be increased in amount but only varied in quality. The mind attains its utmost pleasure in reflecting on the very things that used to cause the greatest mental fears and on things like them.[41]

The presence of women in the garden and the implications of Epicurus' attack on one of his teachers, Nausiphanes,[42] indicate that he disapproved of homosexual love, which in ancient Greece often took the form of a romantic attachment between an older man and a boy or a young man. To the Greeks such a relationship, which came under the term *paederastia,* denoting a sensual and spiritual affection for a boy, was regarded not as a vice but as a normal form of love, even as a supplement to marriage, to be treated as openly as heterosexual love. It needs to be emphasized that in a typical relationship between an older man and a boy the ultimate goals were ethical and intellectual: the older man not only achieved an understanding of the soul of the boy but also inspired and tutored him to come as close as possible to the ideal of the excellent citizen. Essentially, therefore, the Hellenic love of boys was closely related to the ideal of beauty, expressed by the Greek words *kalos kagathos,* or that which is beautiful in body and in soul. That there were shady and unhealthy sides to male homosexuality among the ancient Greeks cannot be denied. "Like the other sort," Kitto notes, "it had its higher and its lower aspect." 43

It is not at all difficult to understand why the young flocked to Epicurus, nor to see why his sayings captured their imagination. Obviously, Epicurus knew how to speak to his young admirers, knew the anguish of their physical desires, and yet knew how to assuage this anguish. Throughout, his words are filled with humility, with sensitivity, with understanding. The period of youth, Epicurus says, is hectic, for "the flesh cries out to be saved from hunger, thirst and cold." It is a period when "the first measure of security is to watch over one's youth and to guard against what makes havoc of all by means of pestering desires." 44 Indeed,

It is not the young man who should be thought happy, but an old man who has lived a good life. For the young man at the height of his powers is unstable and is carried this way and that by fortune, like a headlong stream. But the old man has come to anchor in old age as though in port, and the good things for which before he hardly hoped he has brought into safe harbourage in his grateful recollections.45

But of all Epicurus' words which bespeak his gentle nature and his friendly counsel, none are more memorable than these to a young follower:

You tell me that the stimulus of the flesh makes you too prone to the pleasures of love. Provided that you do not break the laws or good customs and do not distress any of your neighbours or do harm to your body or squander your pittance, you may indulge your inclination as you please. Yet it is impossible not to come up against one or other of these barriers: for the pleasures of love never profited a man and he is lucky if they do him no harm.[46]

Epicurus' views on love were originally given in detail in two of his works now lost, *On Nature* and *On Love,* which Lucretius surely had in mind as he wrote his long discourse on love in Book IV of *On the Nature of Things.*[47] No doubt in this section of Lucretius' poem it is love as practiced in Roman life of the first century B.C. which is reflected. Nonetheless, a quintessentially Epicurean treatment of love pervades the poem, and what Lucretius has to say is most revealing of Epicurus' teachings. Indeed, it is Epicurus' voice that quietly but forcefully echoes in Lucretius' warnings that pain grows with indulgence and that one should avoid "the toils of love" which sap strength and bring no lasting gratification. Lucretius' picture of physical satisfaction's begetting new desire—

At length when the gathered desire has gone forth, there ensues for a brief while a short pause in the burning passion; and then returns the same frenzy, then comes back the old madness, when they are at a loss to know what they really desire to get, and cannot find what device is to conquer that mischief; in such utter uncertainty they pine away by a hidden wound[48]—

recalls Epicurus' contention that "sexual intercourse has never done a man good, and he is lucky if it has not harmed him," [49] and looks ahead to Shakespeare's Sonnet 129, "The expense of spirit in a waste of shame."

VII *"Sweet Friendship"*

Quite clearly Epicurus' approach to friendship was a part of his considerations regarding the whole of man's conduct. The role of physical love must be seen in the light of the Epicurean belief that the pleasures of friendship, arising out of a rational and reflective relation between one person and another, are superior or preferable to the intenser pleasures of love. Tarn goes so far as to describe Epicurus' followers as forming "little isles of quietude apart, bound together by the friendship he so stressed; except that they lived among their fellows and enjoyed family life, one might call them, spiritually, the first monks." [50] This description is entirely warranted, for it is clear that friendship among the Epicureans was an intrinsically religious state, a sacrament in its own right. Epicurus' friends met together in what can be termed a communion of religious feeling, at the basis of which there was a mutuality of religious affection. In their gatherings the Epicureans sought above all else to secure the pleasures of "sweet friendship" (*suavis amicitiae*)—of friendship which achieves the peace which passes all understanding.

"Let us be friends." To the men and women of his time Epicurus spoke these words, which, if they could only conquer, would save the world. The need for friendship in the Hellenistic Age was crucial, for political, social, and religious upheavals had transformed the Greek world. The city-state had given way to the monarchy of Macedon, which eventually fell into chaos with the rule of the successors of Alexander the Great. In Epicurus' time these successors looked on Athens, indeed on Hellas, as just another satrapy. "Their methods and ideas," one scholar sadly points out, "wounded the Hellenic sensibility and soul." [51] Besides, Epicurus' contemporaries lived in the midst of countless fears and superstitions propagated in a welter of religions. An age of vast experiment, it was inevitably an age of instability and insecurity. The world had suddenly become too big and too formless. A human longing to escape such a world was ever-present, and that Epicurus' school provided a refuge is undeniable. "The values of the world," writes Murray, "no longer held good after you had passed the wicket gate of the Garden, and spoken with the Deliverer." [52]

Epicurus did not believe in miracles for the deliverance of mankind. Yet he did believe in the healing powers that friendship brings with it. Friendship was for him the closest thing to miracle. It provided a sense of belonging and a life of dialogue. It made possible in human relationships a depth and a permanence of affections, helping to defeat evil and to overcome unhappiness. Epicurus gave his followers something more than a refuge: he gave them a peaceful home in which they could spend happy days when friendship mastered time itself. Although Epicurus never married, he was the father of a family of friends.

CHAPTER 8

Reputation and Influence

IN HIS own time and in the following centuries Epicurus enjoyed a reputation which fluctuated between opposites: popularity and persecution, love and hatred, worship and denunciation. The spread of his doctrine took place over nearly seven centuries, especially during the years between 300 B.C. and A.D. 150. Nor did it limit its appeal to Athens or even to Greece but in time attracted multitudes in the Greco-Oriental world (*e.g.*, in Antioch, Judaea, and Egypt), in Rome and elsewhere in Italy, and in Roman Africa.

Yet, characteristically, even as Epicureanism prospered, it often had to contend with an opposition that remained neither silent nor even irenic. As Epicurus himself had clashed with the Platonists and the Peripatetics, Epicureanism clashed with Stoicism, first in the person of Chrysippus (d. 206 B.C.), the second founder of Stoicism, and then with Christianity. No matter where Epicureanism appeared, it had to struggle against the suppressive measures of suspicious officials. Although many persons and peoples no doubt welcomed Epicurus' philosophy as a salvation, governing authorities habitually branded it as an enemy that preached individualism, political apathy, irreligion, and pleasure.

Although there were at first periods of success for Epicureanism, there were the inevitable long days of darkness to follow in the Middle Ages, when Epicureanism was equated with the most reprehensible thought and conduct. During the first centuries of the Renaissance, Epicurus was still out of favor: if at all, he was barely mentioned—in whispers. In fact, it can be said that especially after the fifth century Epicureanism incurred more and more the "odour of unsanctity," "named if condemned, unnamed if approved." [1] Many persons of vested interests distrusted Epicurus and wanted to banish him from memory and from history, as they almost did. *Almost*, that is, until the seventeenth century, first in France and then in England, when Epicurus reappeared, even though in fragments.

In Greece in his own time Epicurus made remarkable advances and had "friends, so many in number that they could hardly be counted by whole cities." His teachings earned him the sympathy of the general public and the loyalty of fervent disciples, "held fast . . . by the siren-charms of his doctrine." After his death his doctrine was consolidated and propagated "without interruption through numberless reigns of one scholarch after another." [2] Among those who succeeded Epicurus as head of his school and who, like preachers of the word, passed on his ideas, without violating their purity, were such eminent men as Hermarchus (271–240 B.C.), Polystratus (240–210 B.C.), Dionysius (210–180 B.C.), Basilides (180–150 B.C.), and Apollodorus (150–120 B.C.).

I Greece and Rome

The encounter of Athens and Rome occupies an important, even portentous, place in the history of Epicureanism. This encounter underscores the endurance of Epicureanism, illustrates the innermost significance of its nonconformity, and records its gradual absorption into hardier modes of thinking. At Rome the Greek way of life, with its endemic love of beauty, of philosophy, of contemplation, and of freedom, confronted a way of life that glorified power, organization, obedience, and discipline. A man of action, a warrior, a conqueror for whom war constituted a school for the heroic virtues—this was the famous Roman type that Hellenism confronted. The contrast in cultures is best imaged by the Romans' love of the *munera gladiatoria,* the gladiatorial games that were first held in Rome in 264 B.C. and that continued to be popular with the Roman masses and with leaders like Caesar and Pompey who sought in later years to win the people's favor with games that eventually pitted men against animals. The Greeks, especially Epicurus, would never have tolerated such vulgar spectacles. When an attempt was once made to introduce gladiatorial games into Athens, Demonax, a Cynic philosopher, told the Athenians that they would first have to pull down the altar of Mercy.

It should be recalled that the first encounters of the Romans and the Greeks go back to 700–500 B.C., during the years of Greek colonial expansion in the Mediterranean world, particularly in Sicily and in southern Italy. In the following centuries the Romans often found the Greek way antithetical to theirs. Reasons for their distrust of the Greeks are not difficult to assess. The Romans, Lange reminds us, "valued dominion more than wealth, glory rather than comfort, and triumph more than all. Their virtues were not those of peace, of industrial enterprise, of righteousness, but those of courage, of fortitude, of temperance. The Roman vices were, at least in the beginning, not luxury and wantonness, but hardness, cruelty, and faithlessness." [3]

But as the Romans conquered more and more lands and peoples, it was inevitable that new influences, customs, and ways of life would invade and even captivate Rome itself. Hellenism particularly fascinated the hard, battle-seasoned Romans whose household slaves, teachers, architects, and physicians were usually Greeks. After the Second Punic War (218–201 B.C.) and the defeat of Hannibal at Zama in Africa by Scipio Africanus, Greek culture began to have an increasing influence on the Romans. Greek art and libraries were appropriated by Roman generals and officials. Schools of Greek philosophy and rhetoric were opened, and Greek language and literature were given recognition to the extent that by the last days of the Roman Republic no citizen was considered fully educated unless he had mastered Greek.

II   *Marcus Cato*

If reactions to the gladiatorial games image the differences between the Greek and the Roman ways of life, it is a famous Roman general, consul, and censor, Marcus Cato (234–149 B.C.), who epitomizes the tensions of the Greek and Roman encounter. Uncompromisingly Roman in his love of simplicity and austerity, he was, Plutarch says, "contented with a cold breakfast, a frugal dinner, simple raiment, and a humble dwelling." He even denounced Scipio before the Senate for "waste of enormous moneys, and his boyish addiction to palaestras and theatres, as though he were not commander of an army, but master of a festival." Above all, Cato conceived of himself as a moralist defending Rome's "primitive integrity" against "the hydra-like luxury and effeminacy of the time." [4]

"To watch, admonish, and chastise, that no one should turn aside to wantonness and forsake his native and customary mode of life": these words summarize Cato's aims. In Cato appear the extremes of Roman nationalism and severity that, initially at least, distrusted things Greek. To him admiration of Greek culture represented the Romans' betrayal of "the customs of the fathers." Consequently, he mocked the Hellenophiles among his contemporaries, never failing to comment, "the words of the Greeks were born on their lips, but those of the Romans in their hearts." [5]

When a philosophical mission from Athens visited Rome in 155 B.C. to plead a legal case, the Romans were entranced by the charm and eloquence of the three philosophers who came as representatives: Critolaus the Peripatetic, Diogenes the Stoic, and Carneades the Academic. (There was, alas, no Epicurean representative, perhaps because such an embassy was not in keeping with the Epicurean opposition to public affairs—or perhaps because the other philosophers refused to tolerate an Epicurean colleague.) Carneades especially became so popular that the Roman youth were "possessed" by his eloquence. Their enthusiasm, Plutarch reports, "filled the city, like a rushing mighty wind, with the noise of his praises." [6]

Not unexpectedly Cato was distressed that the Roman youth "should come to love a reputation based on mere words more than one achieved by martial deeds." [7] Practical wisdom, not metaphysics; material achievement, not delicate imagination, Cato insisted, were what Rome needed. Indeed, in 161 B.C. an edict had been passed to prevent philosophers from poisoning the minds of Romans. "Yet nothing—neither senatorial decree nor Catonian fulmination—could check the inrush." [8] Hellenism had come to Rome not as a visitor but as a dweller, even when unwelcomed and hounded by Cato and his band of xenophobiacs. Cato himself could not completely resist the *exemplaria Graeca*: in his last years he devoted himself to studying Greek. Surely his study had some redeeming values, even for one who had screamed out demands in the Roman Senate for the destruction of Carthage!

III *Roman Epicureanism*

Greek philosophy did appeal to the Romans, especially to those of the educated classes. But their usual distrust of things Greek was evident in their belief that it was best "to dip but not to plunge" into Greek thought. What was made clear from the beginning was that the Romans were selective in their use of Greek philosophy, with utilitarian considerations invariably governing their responses: "From the first Rome chose what she would study, modified the tradition she received and thought out her ethics and her politics to suit her own circumstances." [9]

It is difficult to fix the date of the arrival of Epicureanism in Rome, but the fact that in 173 B.C. two Epicureans, Alcaeus and Philiscus, were ordered out of the city would indicate that Epicureanism was not only prevalent in the second century B.C. but even important enough to bring about strong action on the part of the authorities. It is significant, likewise, that the first philosophical work in Latin was written by an older contemporary of Cicero, the Epicurean Gaius Amafinius. The publication of his work was enthusiastically received by the Romans. "The crowd," Cicero records, "had its interest stirred, and flocked to the teaching he advocated in preference to any other, whether because it was so easy to grasp, or because of the seductive allurements of pleasure." [10]

By the first century B.C. Epicureanism was enjoying wide popularity among those Romans who found it refined, decorous, urbane, and charming. There were at least two important reasons for this growing success: First, as a practicing and not an abstract philosophy, Epicureanism appealed to a practical-minded people. And second, in the midst of social turmoil and political unrest, especially after 137 B.C. and the unsuccessful political, agrarian, and judicial reforms first of Tiberius Gracchus and then of his brother Gaius, Epicureanism provided discontented Romans with consolation.

IV   *The First Century B.C.*

The growth of Epicureanism in the first century B.C. was to be more noticeable in the midst of cataclysms like the Social War between Rome and the Italic peoples, 91–89; the Civil War between Gaius Marius and Lucius Cornelius Sulla, 88–82; the war against rebellious slaves led by Spartacus, 73–71; and the Civil War between Caesar and Pompey, 51–48. The Rome of Marius and of Sulla was particularly in a state of unrest and hardship, with tyranny, war, and death ever-present. Surely there were many Romans who must have been repelled when, upon returning to Rome from exile in 87 B.C., Marius, with the support of Cinna the Consul, committed one atrocity after another against his enemies. It was a time of anguish and horror when "every road . . . was filled with men pursuing and hunting down those who sought to escape or had hidden themselves," and "headless trunks thrown into the streets and trampled under foot excited no pity, though everybody trembled and shuddered at the sight." [11]

With the return of Sulla in 82 B.C. the reign of terror was equally heinous.[12] Sulla's famous proscriptions, when lists were issued of persons who could be killed at any time and place, with reward given to the killers, could not be dismissed by the Romans who believed in *humanitas*. It was only natural that some turned to Epicureanism in reaction against a way of life in which slave was slaying master and son slaying father, even as Sulla himself "was proscribing as many as he could remember, and those who now escaped his memory, he would proscribe at a future time." [13] As in Greece during Hellenistic times, there were those who now discovered in Epicureanism a shelter against the crude and vulgar aspects of life as they sought for a philosophical doctrine that opposed the dehumanizing elements of cruelty and war. Epicureanism thus found ready followers among Romans of a quiet and esthetic disposition who were horrified by bloodbaths.

The most notable example of a sensitive Roman who detached himself from the terror and the hatred all around him, "disdainful of all pettiness, preaching apathy with fervour, godlike in his revolt against the gods" is Lucretius.[14] Although strong criticism has been aimed at him for his indifference to the historical urgencies of the Roman world in the first century B.C., such criticism is not justifiable. Lucretius, in refusing to participate in the events of his time, was merely dramatizing the Epicurean disdain for the outer life. He embodied not only Epicurean nonconformity but also Epicurean *ataraxia*. In Lucretius we see a true Epicurean who refused to subordinate philosophical doctrine to the dictates of armed might. His Epicureanism was of the highest kind, nourished and defended in the most extreme of times. A poet of retirement, he represents, as Duff tells us, not only a reflective Epicureanism, but also the serious questioning of his age.

The popularity of Epicureanism in Rome is also attested to by the support and sympathy it received from Calpurnius Piso, the father-in-law of Caesar; from Pomponius Atticus, Cicero's closest friend; from Cassius and Pansa, Caesar's generals; and from Caesar himself. From 70–28 B.C., too, Philodemus, a native of Gadara, Syria, was a very popular Epicurean teacher in Rome and was even admired by Cicero as "an excellent and learned friend." [15]

In their younger days Horace and Virgil were influenced by Epicureanism, both greatly admiring Lucretius' poem. Virgil studied Epicureanism under Siro in the famous garden-school, which the latter directed with Philodemus at Naples and which flourished in the last years of Julius Caesar. Interestingly, Cicero had as one of his first teachers of philosophy an Epicurean, Phaedrus.

V *Cicero's Attacks*

Yet it is Cicero who was Rome's stern and unsparing enemy of Epicureanism and who provides the index both to his age and to the fortunes of Epicureanism. In some ways Cicero's attacks on Epicurus were indicative of a perpetual Roman suspicion of the Greeks. Cicero personifies the syncretistic Roman temper, always appreciative of Greek accomplishments in art, in literature, and in philosophy, but at the same time aware of the Romans' distinctive worth and destiny. "For morality, rules of life, family and household economy," Cicero insists, "are surely maintained by us in a better and more dignified way [than by the Greeks]; and beyond question our ancestors have adopted better regulations and laws than others in directing the policy of government. . . . Where has such earnestness . . . such firmness, greatness of soul, honesty, loyalty . . . such surpassing merit in every field been found in any of mankind to justify comparison with our ancestors?" [16]

In the light of these feelings, we can understand why Cicero condemned Epicureanism. Epicurus' teachings, he thought, ruin all virtue and "pervert all duty." Against the Epicureans, he says, "we must fight with man and horse . . . if it is our intention to defend and retain virtue." In particular he criticized Epicurus' concept of pleasure, saying: "For how can he commend temperance who places the chief good in pleasure? For temperance is hostile to irregular passions; but irregular passions are the companions of pleasure." [17] Furthermore, Cicero felt that Epicureanism corrupted Roman lives "with bowered seclusion, luxury, ease, indolence, and sloth." [18] But worst of all, it taught that one should avoid public life and service. To the Romans, certainly, such forbearance constituted treason.

In his speech against Lucius Calpurnius Piso, delivered before the Roman Senate in 55 B.C., Cicero censured Caesar's father-in-law for misgovernment of the province of Macedonia. Implicitly and explicitly his harangue against Piso was couched in an anti-

Epicurean idiom, anticipating the kind of invective that in the centuries to follow would constantly be used. Piso was said to embody the lowest Epicurean traits: he was "a debauchee [who] lolled amid his tipsy and malodorous Greeks," immersed in a "miserable slough of degradation." In "this Epicurus of mud and clay" there could be found "no good taste, no refinement, no elegance": "he is the last word in voluptuousness, in licentiousness, in baseness, in villainy." [19]

Above all, Cicero made Piso out as the foolish victim of Epicurean doctrine propounded by Philodemus, the Epicurean teacher befriended by Piso. (It should be noted that Cicero credited Philodemus with paying attention to literature, in contrast to most Epicureans, who neglected it.) For Cicero, Piso served as a primary example of a man who had been corrupted by Epicurean philosophy—"a dangerous argument to put before a young man of only moderate intelligence, and one that often leads to disaster." [20] To the question of why such a person could go wrong, Cicero's reply was that it was Epicurus' fault for misleading those who would listen to his counsel. Look at poor Piso, Cicero seems to be saying: having "heard pleasure praised so highly by so great a philosopher, he did not pick and choose; he so stimulated all his pleasurable sensations, and raised such a whinnying to welcome his friend's arguments, that he plainly thought he had found in the Greek not a professor of ethics but a master of the art of lust." [21]

In his attacks Cicero irreparably damaged the reputation and the fate of Epicureanism. Preparing the way for the eventual silencing of Epicurean adherents after the third century, he provided the vocabulary of vituperation for their opponents. He incorporated in his writings the misrepresentation that ultimately became a permanent part of the history of Epicureanism. For many, many centuries after Cicero, Epicureanism was equated with unbridled hedonism; and Cicero's writings were often the source of this attitude.

VI *The Roman Empire*

Under the Roman Republic, nevertheless, Epicureanism made its way in spite of the attacks against it. Portraits and statues of Epicurus were very popular among Roman Epicureans, who even displayed likenesses of him in their bedrooms and on their drinking cups and rings. This popularity continued after the beginning of one-man rule by Caesar Augustus in 31 B.C. During the first and second centuries of the Roman Empire, Epicureanism managed to hold its own. Among the Romans of these times it was popular chiefly with those who opposed the superstition and the mysticism drifting into Rome. Outside of Rome the extent of its influence is evidenced in one way or another by its wide popularity in Asia Minor (we can recall here Alexander the False Prophet and his attempts to stamp out the Epicureans) and by the missionary zeal of an Epicurean teacher like Diogenes of Oenoanda, also in Asia Minor. Epicurean circles, in other words, were active even in the midst of Roman totalitarianism and the popular mystical religions arising in the East—the cults of Mithras the Persian god, of Isis the Egyptian goddess, and of Jesus Christ.

On the whole, however, Epicureanism was waning in the days of the Roman Empire, no matter what spasmodic fame it enjoyed. By the fourth century it had all but disappeared as an organized movement. The Emperor Julian, for example, who reigned 361–363, pinpoints this disappearance in saying: "But indeed the gods have already in their wisdom destroyed [Epicurus'] works, so that most of [his] books have ceased to be." [22] And later on Saint Augustine, speaking of this demise, notes that "their contentions have been rooted out and reduced to silence." [23]

Epicureanism failed to survive in the Roman Empire precisely because these were times when cultural retrenchment became the most conspicuous characteristic of Roman life and thought. From the reign of Augustus, the religious ideals of the Roman past were revived, as seen in the restoration of temples, in the interest in ancestor-worship, in the resumption of old rites and ceremonies, in the reform and re-establishment of state priesthoods. Again from the reign of Augustus, emperor-worship became prevalent. Augustus himself was not only a *princeps* but also a *pater patriae,* a *pontifex maximus,* a *divi filius.* Hence, the temper of the Roman Empire was basically inimical to Epicurean philosophy, with its emphasis on tranquillity, on contemplation, on individualism, on personal relationships, on friendship. These elements were no doubt seen as threats to the powers of the state and of the emperor. At any time and in any society such emphasis can be but a potential threat to dictatorship and to the power of the few.

The Roman Empire marked the triumph of organization and

absolutism—political, military, religious. The humanism and the sensitivity sacred to Epicureanism could not possibly survive in such an atmosphere. Empires and police states are not founded on friendship, nor do they endure by depending on sensitizing experiences. Rather, their main requisitions are toughness, fortitude, drive, allegiance to authority, and unswerving devotion to duty— the execution of the task that Epictetus, a celebrated Stoic exponent and a teacher of the Emperor Marcus Aurelius (who reigned 161–180), recognized as the refusal to "desert this post as long as it is assigned to me." These elements alone nourish an empire.

VII Epicureanism and the Spread of Christianity

The demise of Epicureanism was to be concurrent with the growth of Christianity, especially in the years after the death of Marcus Aurelius in 180. In the early days of the Roman Empire, to recall, there was hostility toward the Christians, who were looked on as politically dangerous. During the reigns of Nero and Domitian, brutal persecutions of the Christians took place. In the second century, however, the lot of the Christians under the "good Emperors" like Trajan, Hadrian, and Antoninus Pius was somewhat improved. Then, in the fourth century, especially 303–311, the burning of holy books, the destruction of churches, the imprisonment and slaughter of Christian believers characterized new persecutions, carried on by the Emperor Diocletian. Nevertheless, after the Emperor Constantine's Edict of Milan in 313, proclaiming religious toleration and granting Christianity equality with paganism, Christianity not only became more and more accepted but also became a powerful cultural influence. Edward Gibbon, in the celebrated fifteenth chapter of The Decline and Fall of the Roman Empire, describes the advance of Christianity and the gradual collapse of the Empire in these words:

While that great body was invaded by open violence, or undermined by slow decay, a pure and humble religion gently insinuated itself into the minds of men, grew up in silence and obscurity, derived new vigor from opposition, and finally erected the triumphant banner of the cross on the ruins of the Capitol.

For some Christians ancient philosophy was always suspect of heretical tendencies. Tertullian (*ca.* 160–*ca.* 220), who is placed next to Augustine as the greatest Western theologian of the patristic period and who was the first theologian to write in Latin, shows a strong distrust of all philosophy and condemns the restless minds and the curiosity of heretics. In one of his writings, *On Prescription Against Heretics,* Tertullian emphasizes that "heresies are themselves instigated by philosophy." "What indeed," he cries, "has Athens to do with Jerusalem?" For, he adds, "with our faith we desire no further belief," even as "we want no curious disputation after possessing Christ Jesus." Pagan philosophy, he insists, is a "vain deceit," a perversion of truth, incompatible with Christian belief and dogma.[24]

In the Western Church religious thinkers and leaders like Arnobius, Saint Ambrose, Tertullian, Saint Jerome, and Saint Gregory considered pagan learning profane and potentially heretical. It should be noted here that the early Latin theologians differed from the Greek theologians, who liked to affirm their Hellenist traditions and saw a philosopher like Plato as a precursor of Christ. In contrast with Augustine, who declared, "It is one thing from the woody top of a mountain to see the land of peace, and not to find the way thither" [25]—a statement that indicts purely philosophical speculations and quests—a Greek father of the Church, Clement of Alexandria, looked on philosophy as purging the soul and preparing it for the reception of faith, "on which the Truth builds up the edifice of knowledge." [26] In any event, the Christian Church in the West was always on guard against heretical tendencies in any philosophical system and inevitably associated a philosopher like Epicurus with heresy. Characteristic of its early teachings was the need to refute "the folly of Epicurus," a *voluptarius* who had denied divine creation and the immortality of the soul.

Lactantius (*ca.* 240–*ca.* 320), a Latin apologist known as the "Christian Cicero," mirrors the Christians' detestation of Epicurus. Insisting on divine creation, Lactantius ridiculed Epicurean theology and atomism. In his attempt to refute Epicurus, he stressed that to abandon the idea of divine providence destroys religion and results in confusion. Epicurus, according to Lactantius, is not only a heretic who contributes to the breakdown of faith but also a demagogic philosopher who promises everything to everyone. In the following passage from *The Divine Institutes*, Lactantius displays the subtle powers that made him a famous rhetorician. At the same time, he discloses the Christians' suspicion of Epicurus:

Moreover, for the purpose of drawing the multitude to himself, he speaks that which is specially adapted to each character separately. He forbids the idle to apply himself to learning; he releases the covetous man from giving largesses to people; he prohibits the inactive man from undertaking the business of the state, the sluggish from bodily exercise, the timid from military service. The irreligious is told that the gods pay no attention to the conduct of men; the man who is unfeeling and selfish is ordered to give nothing to any one, for the wise man does everything on his own account. To a man who avoids the crowd, solitude is praised. One who is too sparing, learns that life can be sustained on water and meal. If a man hates his wife, the blessings of celibacy are enumerated to him; to one who has bad children, the happiness of those who are without children is proclaimed; against unnatural parents it is said that there is no bond of nature. To the man who is delicate and incapable of endurance, it is said that pain is the greatest of all evils; to the man of fortitude, it is said that the wise man is happy even under tortures. The man who devotes himself to the pursuit of influence and distinction is enjoined to pay court to kings; he who cannot endure annoyance is enjoined to shun the abode of kings.[27]

VIII *The Middle Ages*

In the light of the Christians' view of Epicurus as a heretic, it is not difficult to understand why his philosophy was eclipsed during the thousand years we call the Middle Ages. During this phase of Western civilization Epicurus was viewed as an infamous figure: an atheist, a hedonist, an anti-Christ, an arch-rejector of the truth of the *sacramentum mundi et hominum*. He became a stereotype of sensuality: In Martianus Capella's *Nuptials of Mercury and Philology*, Epicurus appears bearing roses and violets and all manner of enticements to pleasure ("Epicurus vero mixtas violis rosas et totas apportabat inlecebras voluptatum").

In an age when the badge of faith was necessary to one striving to remain in "the hands of God" and when the mystery of eternal life was of primary concern, Epicurus could hardly find a sympathetic following. He had no place in a society agonized by what Dawson terms "the eschatological dualism of the present world and the world to come which was the background of the medieval Christian view of life." [28] This was a time for pilgrims and pilgrimages, for the glorification of saints and martyrs; it was not a time for a philosophy that denied the immortality of the soul and, in Augustine's phrase, "the eternal repose not only of the spirit, but also of the body."

The medieval scorn of Epicurus is crystallized in Dante's *Divine Comedy*, especially in the ninth and tenth cantos of the *Inferno*, where Dante treats Epicurus and his followers as heretics. Dante dramatizes the ultimate penalty to be suffered by those who, like Epicurus, deny God and eternal life. He places them in the sixth circle of hell—in "a plain, stretched spacious on both sides,/Filled with ill woes and torments desolate." They are to be found in countless, half-opened, burning tombs, "so white-hot as never burned/Iron in the forge of any artificers." From within these tombs come forth "fearful crying" and "sad sighing." As Virgil then informs Dante, "All these shall be shut fast and sealed/When from Jehoshaphat [the valley where the Last Judgment will occur] they come anew,/Bringing their bodies now left far afield." [29] It is worth noting that Epicurus is placed among the heretics of Christian times, for he, almost alone among pagan philosophers, denied the soul's immortality.

For a thousand years the Christian Church was successful in burying Epicurus in a sepulchre in hell. The reasons for the violent opposition to him, as already seen, make it clear that his philosophical doctrine signified to the Christian believer the victory of an earthly city over the "city to come," the city of God. Consequently, the Christians anathematized Epicurus when necessary and consigned him to anonymity when possible. Yet any reasonable comparison of Epicurean philosophy, rooted in the need to effect communion between men, and the Christian religion, rooted in the need to attain communion with God, must ultimately point to some remarkable if subtle parallels. Not without significance is the fact that Augustine once thought highly of Epicurus and would have awarded him the garland, "had I not verily believed that there remained a life for the soul after the body was dead, and the fruits of our deservings, which Epicurus would not believe." [30] According to Augustine, the Epicureans possessed many virtues, but because of their denial of divine creation and of the immortality of the soul, they could never participate in the mystery of salvation or attain the vision "of the eternal felicity of

God and of the perpetual Sabbath": that "eighth and eternal day" when mankind "shall rest and see, see and love, love and praise. This is what shall be in the end without end. For what other end do we propose to ourselves than to attain to the kingdom of which there is no end?"

IX   Resemblances between Epicureans and Christians

If the Epicureans could not share with the Christians in the mystery of redemption, or if they were neither members of the "One Body," the "Body of Christ," nor "a chosen race, a royal priesthood, a holy nation, a people set apart" [31]—that faithful "little flock" to which it was God's "good pleasure to give . . . the kingdom" [32]—they nevertheless followed a pattern of conduct which the Christians also followed and for which they often sacrificed their lives. Indeed, the Christian counsels of humility, tenderness, mercy, patience, endurance, and love were prefigured hundreds of years earlier in the counsels of Epicurus. In its ethical precepts Christianity constituted a transformed, a divinized Epicureanism. Both were missionary and devotional religions; both were dogmatic and proselytizing; both condemned deceit, arrogance, glory, wealth, and power. Their formal observances, for example, their use of ritual and their celebration of holy days; their dogmatic philosophy and foundations of faith—the Epicureans with their handbooks and "authorized doctrines," the Christians with their Articles of Faith; their distrust of "public affairs" and their essentially autonomous position outside society; their communal meetings in private houses, their hierarchical organization, their devotional readings and meditations; their emphasis on free will; their rejection of all divination and oracles; their epistolary exhortations: surely these are resemblances that cannot be overlooked by even the most zealous Christian enemy of Epicurus.

In *St. Paul and Epicurus,* DeWitt argues that Epicurus acted as a bridge from Greek philosophy to the Christian religion, from a philosophy of hope to a religion of hope. In particular the writings of Saint Paul, he tries to show, were influenced by Epicurus, for "both his [Paul's] ideology and his terminology reveal unmistakable recollections of known sayings of Epicurus." [33] As DeWitt brings out in support of his thesis, Epicureanism flourished in Tarsus and Antioch during the first century B.C. That Epicurus' teachings were popular could not have escaped Paul's awareness. Though he was repelled by the Epicurean doctrine of pleasure, Paul found "the tidy reasonings" of Epicurus attractive, and the merit of Epicurus' ethic "was so superior and so widely acknowledged that Paul had no alternative but to adopt it and bless it with the new sanction of religion." [34] Thus Christianity sometimes viewed Epicureanism with a mixture of detestation and admiration. Christians like Paul undoubtedly recognized, though they did not acknowledge, some of the merits of Epicurus' ethical teachings and did not hesitate to absorb them.

In their asceticism and in their fervor, too, the Epicureans anticipated the Christians. It would not be excessive to say that the Epicureans, like the Christians, were persecuted witnesses to a dogmatic philosophy. But because Epicurus' vision of life was limited by its secularism, for it emptied the universe of God, the Christians looked on Epicureanism as enunciating a bold form of religious suprasufficiency, which not only denied God but also made the ministry of Jesus Christ unnecessary. Hence, Epicureanism represented an irredeemable heresy, alien to the apocalyptic faith of the Christians. In short, though Epicureanism possessed many distinctly religious dimensions, it lacked the consecrating grace that the Christians associated with the ultimate religious dimension, the eschatological dimension: the four "last things"—death, judgment, heaven, and hell.

X *Awakening Interest*

By and large the entombment of Epicureanism continued until the sixteenth century. In 1523 Diogenes Laertius' work was printed in Basel and was eventually reprinted many times. Earlier, in 1473, Lucretius' poem had been printed in Brescia; by 1650 this edition had been reissued thirty-four times by continental presses. The printings of these *editiones principes* obviously played an important role not only in awakening interest in Epicureanism but also in making primary Epicurean texts available. As a result, Epicurean theories gradually exerted their influence on thinkers who questioned metaphysical speculations, or who disagreed with Aristotle, or who could not accept orthodox religious tenets. Such a nonconformist thinker was Giordano Bruno (1548–1600), who had to leave the Dominican order for harboring beliefs that smacked of Epicureanism, particularly that the universe is infinite in time and space and that the solar system is one of innumerable worlds. For these beliefs he had returned to Epicurus and to Lucretius. Arrested by the Inquisition, Bruno was imprisoned and was burned at the stake on February 17, 1600.

XI *Pierre Gassendi and the Epicurean Revival*

Ironically, it was a Roman Catholic priest, Provost of the Cathedral at Digne in Provence, France, who inaugurated a powerful Epicurean revival in the seventeenth century and who can even be considered as the propagator of modern materialism. This priest was Pierre Gassendi (1592–1655), a devout Franciscan, a mathematician, a scientist, and a philosopher. Opposed to Aristotelianism, he championed the theory of atomism and considered Democritus and Epicurus as the greatest ancient philosophers. Two works of Gassendi were important in reviving and re-evaluating Epicurus' ideas: *De vita et moribus Epicuri* (1647) and *Animadversiones in decimum librum Diogenis Laërtii, qui est de vita, moribus placitisque Epicuri*, with *Philosophiae Epicuri syntagma* as an appendix (1649). Gassendi presented Epicurus as a man of vision and character. Seeking above all to vindicate Epicurus' moral teachings, he embraced at the same time Epicurus' atomism, which he united with Christian theology, saying that the original motion of the atoms was directed by God and that the development of all things was a reflection of the will of God.

Of course, Gassendi did not accept all of Epicurus' doctrines, for example, the rejection of divine providence and of the immortality of the soul. However, he stressed that Epicurus' attack against superstition and the religion of his age was commendable. Epicurus simply did not know the true religion. Gassendi was greatly effective in exonerating Epicurus from the charges which had been leveled against him for many centuries, and his work was of inestimable importance in the disentombment of Epicureanism, especially as his interpretations attracted considerable attention outside of France. "Atomism, by *his* means drawn again from antiquity," Lange asserts, "attained a lasting importance, however much it was gradually modified as it passed through the hands of later inquirers." [35]

XII   *Seventeenth-Century England*

In seventeenth-century England Gassendi's revival of Epicurean-ism was to arouse responses—favorable, unfavorable, and ambiv-alent—as his ideas gained circulation. These differing responses were symptomatic of the sharp ideological tensions existing be-tween the old authority and an emerging scientific spirit. In Eng-land it was a century of crisis, instigated by a mood of inquiry. The development of the "new philosophy" was characterized by a suspicion of divine mystery, by a growing rejection of scholasti-cism, with its metaphysical, theological, and teleological orienta-tions, and by a concentration on reason, on science, on methodical investigation and experimentation. The old values, the old reli-gious beliefs, the old faith were now no longer unquestioned. The "new philosophy" presented a challenge to the old, especially to the postulate "that the universe had been fashioned by a personal God who had revealed Himself to men in specific ways; and [to] the metaphysical doctrines of being, creation, becoming, and end, [which] were consequences of this postulate." [36]

Before the seventeenth century the English employed the word "Epicure" as a synonym for a profligate and an atheist. That Epi-curus was an opprobrious philosopher was assumed by those Eng-lishmen who knew of him through Cicero, Augustine, and Lac-tantius. Suspicion of Epicurus was evidenced by an incomplete English translation of Diogenes Laertius by William Baldewyn, published *ca.* 1550—a work which omitted any reference to the Greek atomists. In 1615 Thomas Palfreyman published a revision of Baldewyn's work which included a brief biographical sketch of Democritus, but it made no mention of Epicurus. (Not until 1688 was Diogenes Laertius' complete work, including Book X, which contains the life and philosophy of Epicurus, translated into Eng-lish "By Several Hands.") Of course, Epicurus was not without his enemies in the English churches, including famous preachers like Lancelot Andrewes (1555–1626) and Joseph Hall (1574–1656), who attacked him for denying the immortality of the soul. The publication of a treatise in 1604 "against atheists, Epicures, pay-nims, Jews, Mahometists, and other infidels" [37] is a telling indica-tion of the official hostility against him.

Yet the emergence in the first half of the seventeenth century of the "new philosophy" accounted for some sympathetic responses to Epicurus that the ecclesiastics could not completely annihilate. Francis Bacon (1561–1626), one of the most famous "restorers of philosophy," certainly shows a sympathy with Epicurus. Thus, in his essay "Of Atheism" he terms Epicurus "noble and divine" and defends him against the charge of atheism: "Nay, even that school which is most accused of atheism doth most demonstrate religion; that is, the school of Leucippus and Democritus and Epicurus." Although critical of his presupposed atheism, Robert Burton (1577–1640) is not averse to praising the "temperate" Epicurus and to echoing in the section "Against Sorrow for Death of Friends or otherwise, vain Fear, etc." in *The Anatomy of Melancholy* some Epicurean utterances concerning mortality. Then, too, there is the sensitive appreciation by Sir Thomas Browne (1605–82) in his *Vulgar Errors* (1646). To Browne "the vertuous Epicurus" and the "true Epicurism" offer a guide to practical conduct. Strongly sympathizing with Epicurus' moral philosophy, he blames Cicero, Plutarch, Ambrose, and the Stoics for their misrepresentation of it. "The ground hereof," he states, "seems a misapprehension of his opinion, who placed his Felicity not in the pleasures of the body, but the mind, and tranquility thereof, obtained by wisdom and vertue, as is clearly determined in his Epistle to Menaeceus." [38]

XIII   *Walter Charleton*

The years between 1650 and 1725 witnessed an Epicurean resurgence in English life and letters. The turning point of Epicurus' reputation was 1656, which saw the publication of Walter Charleton's *Epicurus's Morals*. (This year also marked the first publication of an English fragmentary translation of Lucretius, John Evelyn's *An Essay on the First Book of T. Lucretius Carus' De Rerum Natura Interpreted and Made English Verse*. The first complete English verse translation of Lucretius, by Thomas Creech, was published at Oxford in 1682.) Charleton, a medical doctor well-read in the ancients, had been introduced to Gassendi's work by his friend Thomas Hobbes. Charleton's book, subtitled *Collected Partly out of his own Greek text, in Diogenes Laertius, and Partly out of the Rhapsodies of Marcus Antoninus, Plutarch, Cicero, and Seneca*, was "the closest approach made by an English scholar in the early days of the new philosophy to the voluminous *Syntagma* of Gassendi." [39] Through this volume Charleton made available to both specialist and nonspecialist readers "faithfully Englished" translations of Epicurean texts.

Epicurus's Morals is a presentation of his moral doctrine (his atomism is ignored), which is given the form of direct utterance by Epicurus. As Charleton notes, "Epicurus has now learn'd English on purpose to converse more familiarly with you." Terming him "a sublime Wit, a profound Judgement, and a great Master of Temperance, Sobriety, Continence, Fortitude and all other Virtues," Charleton in his preface, "An Apology for Epicurus," defends him against the "odium and infamy" occasioned by his committing "three capital crimes," that is, his denial of the immortality of the soul, his rejection of divine providence, and his justification of suicide. Any one of these positions, Charleton argues, is defensible and reasonable when one considers the times in which Epicurus lived, and by no means can he be called "Atheist, Impious Wretch, Secretary to Hell, Enemy to all Religion." Charleton's work, it is held, "was the first orderly exposition of the ethic of Epicurus in any modern language." [40]

XIV *Thomas Hobbes*

The impact of Epicureanism on English philosophy was undoubtedly powerful, especially as seen in Thomas Hobbes (1588–1679). Hobbes did not recognize either Epicurus or Lucretius by name, but his philosophy reflects a strong grasp of Epicurean ideas. From 1640 to 1651 Hobbes lived in Paris, where he knew Gassendi, a professor of mathematics at the Collège Royal since 1645. This acquaintanceship brought Hobbes into touch with the philosophy of Epicurus. That Hobbes did not accept the principles of atomism and of free will, that he remained a determinist, and that he believed the universe to be a "plenum" are basic differences separating him from Epicurus. But that there are a similarity and a sympathy of temper in the two would indicate that the Englishman knew and profited from the Greek. Although their philosophical viewpoints were not identical, they were certainly congenial.

From the outset one kind of reaction to Hobbes was reminiscent of one to Epicurus. For his *Leviathan* (1651), Hobbes was indicted on the grounds of irreligion, licentiousness, and impiety, charges that had long dogged Epicurus. Indeed, Hobbism was attacked for the same reasons that Epicureanism had been: for its concept of religion as the outgrowth of terror and superstition; for its criticisms of the defenders of "Aristotelity"; for its repudiation of a separate, immaterial soul; for its stress on materialism. Indeed, too, as vituperation was always a distinct feature of some reactions to Epicurus, Hobbes was not without his traducers. A contemporary, Ralph Cudworth, condemned his "new model of ethics which hath been obtruded upon the world with such fatuosity." [41] And in recent times T. S. Eliot has spoken of Hobbes as "one of those extraordinary little upstarts whom the chaotic motions of the Renaissance tossed into an eminence which they hardly deserved and have never lost." [42]

In Hobbes, Epicurus was to have an inheritor of some of his basic views. "His thought," Mayo observes, "thus shared with revived Epicureanism the radical position in the intellectual alignment of seventeenth century England." [43] In many ways Hobbism was a metamorphosed Epicureanism, though one that was much harder and sterner and systematized in tone and approach: a non-idealized Epicureanism, so to speak, preoccupied not with the individual life but with the social life—exalting the state over the individual, converting even religion to the needs of the state, giving supreme power to an absolute sovereign, in so far as "the problem of society becomes the problem of authority." [44] The desire for peace and stability are no less Hobbes's than Epicurus'. But now the Epicurean *soter* is transformed into an absolute sovereign who makes all decisions concerning right or wrong in a world in which the war "of every man against every man" is a natural state to be controlled by reason and authority. Hobbism is a modernized, technocratic Epicureanism. Hobbism is a sunless Epicureanism.

XV *Ambivalent Reactions*

The Epicurean revival in England during the seventeenth century often aroused qualified enthusiasm. For example, a physicist and chemist like Robert Boyle (1627–91), under the influence of Gassendi, applauded Epicurus' moral philosophy and appreciated his study of nature. But, as others were to do not only in the seventeenth but also in the eighteenth century, Boyle reproved Epicurean theology and refused to give up faith in an omnipotent deity, defending "the excellency of theology, compared with natural philosophy." Similarly, clergymen like Joseph Glanvill (1636–80) and Thomas Tenison (1636–1715) accepted the scientific aspects of Epicureanism and hailed the revival of the ancient atomists. Glanvill wrote: "Thus the *Aristotelian Philosophy* hath prevailed; while the more excellent *Hypotheses of Democritus* and *Epicurus* have long lain buryed under neglect and obloquy: and for ought I know might have slept for ever, had not the ingenuity of this age recall'd them from their *Urne*." [45] And yet, though these men were willing to accept Epicurean science, they vehemently opposed Epicurus the "atheist" and his heir, Hobbes, "the person who endeavoureth to shake the Foundations of Religion."

English literature, especially in the second half of the seventeenth century, showed the marks of Epicureanism. Restoration dramatists like Sir George Etheridge (1635?–91?), William Wycherley (1640–1716), and William Congreve (1670–1729) reflected the tone of the Epicurean revival. A poet like Abraham Cowley (1618–67) revealed the Epicureanism of Gassendi and Charleton, Epicureanism "rightly understood." A Christianized Epicurean, Cowley disclosed his admiration for Epicurus in his *Essays, in Verse and Prose.* Certainly, Cowley's observation that "What a brave Privilege is it to be free from all Contentions, from all Envying or being Envyed" [46] and his tribute in lines like the following,

> When *Epicurus* to the World had taught,
> 　That Pleasure was the chiefest Good,
> (And was perhaps i'th'right, if rightly understood)
> 　His life he to his Doctrine brought,
> And in a Gardens shade that Sovereign Pleasure sought:
> Whoever a true Epicure would be,
> May there find cheap and virtuous Luxurie,

indicate a sympathetic grasp of Epicurean thought. And lines like these in his well-known poem "The Wish,"

> Ah, yet, ere I descend to the grave,
> May I a small house and large garden have;
> And a few friends, and many books, both true,
> Both wise, and both delightful too!

disclose familiar Epicurean echoes. Undoubtedly, too, John Dryden (1631–1700), poet laureate and literary dictator of his age, did a great deal to popularize Epicureanism when in 1685 there appeared in his *Second Miscellany* some verse translations of various passages from Lucretius. Although he attacked Epicurean theology as being "absurd," Dryden admired Lucretius' "sublime and daring genius" and his "lofty expressions."

XVI *Opposition*

Usually inherent in the reactions to Epicureanism in England (and everywhere else, for that matter) was a suspicion of Epicurus' theology. Even when Englishmen admired Epicurus as a moral philosopher and as an atomist, they were unwilling to sanction his theology, chiefly because of its denial of divine providence and of the immortality of the soul. Hence, attacks on the "mechanical-atheistic" views of "Epicurean scorners," on "the Epicurean herd of brutish men," and on "the furious fancies of Epicurism and atheism" at times reached unwarranted proportions. The incompatibility of Epicurus' theology and Christian theology was always at the root of these attacks. Richard Bentley (1662–1742), a clergyman and scholar, illustrates the equating of Epicurus with atheism and immorality. In eight sermons given as the Boyle Lectures in 1692, under the title "The Folly and Unreasonableness of Atheism," he indicted Epicurus as the "old master" of the atheists and Epicurus' gods as being "dissolved in laziness and ease." The title of Bentley's lectures in many ways summarizes the hostility to Epicureanism not only in English learned circles but also among the English middle class, with its strongly Puritanical tradition and its emphasis on commercial and worldly success.

By far the most virulent campaign carried on against Epicureanism was that of a group of seventeenth-century English divines known as the Cambridge Platonists, who included Benjamin Whichcote (1609–83), Henry More (1614–87), John Smith (1616?–52), Ralph Cudworth (1617–88), and John Worthington (1618–71). To formulate a philosophy of religion and to stress the divine inspiration of human reason, to prove the reality of the incorporeal in opposition to the new materialism and skepticism, to show that there is one perfect mind which is the source of all truth and value, a Divine Archetype, completely good and pure, that men should aspire to and imitate—these were the chief goals of

Cambridge Platonism. Understandably, then, its adherents looked on the Epicurean revival as a serious threat to orthodox Christian belief and tradition, for in Epicureanism they saw a three-headed monster: materialism, determinism, and atheism. Consequently, to the Cambridge Platonists, who believed that "the spirit of man is the candle of the Lord," Epicurus was "the absolute atheist" and Hobbes was responsible for bringing back the "Epicurean heresy."

The writings of Henry More, described by his seventeenth-century biographer as a "shining light" and a "Celestial Herald," illustrate the Cambridge Platonists' "Holy War" against Epicureanism and Hobbism. In works like *Antidote against Atheism* and *Treatise of the Immortality of the Soul,* More sought to refute Epicurean theology. Returning to the philosophy of Plato and of Plotinus for support against Epicurean theology in general and Hobbism in particular, he insisted that "there is an inseparable Idea of Being absolutely Perfect ever residing, though not always acting, in the Soul of Man." God's wisdom, he maintained, is everywhere and eternal: "Wherefore the whole Creation in general and every part thereof being so ordered as if the most exquisite Reason and Knowledge had contrived them, it is as natural to conclude that all this is the work of a Wise God. . . ." [47] In verse, too, More mused: "I come from Heaven; am an immortal Ray/of God; O Joy! and back to God shall goe." [48] No words could better express the teleological views of the Cambridge Platonists, nor indicate the immense distance separating them from Epicureanism.

XVII *The Eighteenth Century*

During the eighteenth century Epicurus did not receive the acceptance one would expect in a period known as the Enlightenment. Even when notice of him was taken, it was a blend of praise and censure, more the latter than otherwise. The reason for this deficiency is underscored by Hadzsits, who writes: "Atomism signified a denial of a supreme, intelligent Power, it meant 'atheism,' it destroyed belief in immortality: these conclusions were more than the eighteenth century could swallow." [49] The deists were critical of Epicurus in so far as he denied the doctrine of a divine design of the universe, and the celebrated French philosopher Voltaire (1694–1778) had mixed opinions. "A great supporter of a purified teleology" to whom "God is a deliberating artist who has created the world according to reasons of wise purpose," [50] Voltaire could scarcely admire Epicurus' concept of the gods, though he no doubt shared Epicurus' disdain for ecclesiastical religion as an offshoot of fear and superstition. Hence, Epicurus was for Voltaire "a very bad natural philosopher" and one who was also to be reprimanded for advocating withdrawal from life. On the other hand, Voltaire liked "true" Epicurean ethics and felt that Epicurus himself was a good man who "carefully taught the principles of benignity, temperance, moderation, and justice." [51]

In eighteenth-century England the Epicurean revival had fizzled out, and anti-Epicurean sentiments were now prevalent not only in the literary world of Addison, Pope, and Swift, but also in the philosophical world of Shaftesbury, who believed in a benevolent cosmic order, and of Bishop Berkeley, who fought against "Scepticism, Atheism, and Irreligion." There appeared in 1712 an anti-Epicurean poem by Sir Richard Blackmore entitled *Creation; a philosophical Poem demonstrating the Existence and Providence of God.* The preface contains these words: "But among all the ancient obdurate atheists and inveterate enemies of religion, no one seems more sincere, or more implacable, than Epicurus."

Joseph Addison, who hated all "bigoted infidels," praised Blackmore's poem in the *Spectator* (No. 339; March 29, 1712), declaring that "it deserves to be looked upon as one of the most useful and noble productions in our English verse." And Dr. Johnson termed it "one of the first favourites of the English Muse." Jonathan Swift, especially after *The Tale of the Tub,* was another opponent of Epicureanism. In his *Thoughts on Various Subjects* his feelings against the Epicureans are given vent in a passage like this: "The Epicureans began to spread at Rome in the empire of Augustus, as the Socinians and even the Epicureans, too, did in England toward the end of King Charles the Second's reign. . . . They both seemed to be corruptions occasioned by luxury and peace, and by politeness beginning to decline."

XVIII   *The Nineteenth Century to the Present*

In the nineteenth century Epicureanism fared better. In a century characterized by its stress on utilitarianism, on "universalistic hedonism," and on liberalism, when the impelling spirit of philosophy was essentially anti-Platonic, Epicurean attitudes were attractive. Metaphysical knowledge and traditional theology gave way more and more to the need, as Carré writes, to base answers on "external nature and to seek there not magical powers but material fruits that would confer manifold benefits upon men." [52] (Karl Marx, it is interesting to note, wrote his doctoral dissertation on *The Difference Between the Democritean and Epicurean Philosophies of Nature,* which he presented at the University of Jena in 1841.) Happiness, freedom, and security now constituted the desired ends of life, precisely those desiderata that Epicurus emphasized in his garden many centuries before. In the utilitarian movement Jeremy Bentham and John Stuart Mill stand out as leaders, though their concern for the general good or for happiness as the end of law and of morality was undoubtedly anticipated in various ways by Leibniz in Germany, by eighteenth-century French materialists like Helvétius, Montesquieu, and Von Holbach, and by English philosophers like Bacon, Hobbes, Locke, and Hume. Behind this utilitarian speculation, with its criticism of the abuses of custom and with its pleas for moral, political, and social reform, was, as DeWitt puts it, the "fertile seed of Epicureanism." [53]

The Epicurean disdain for absolute authority and the emphasis on the pursuit of happiness and the demand for minimal government were manifest in the New World in the views of Thomas Jefferson (1743–1826), who considered himself an Epicurean and who studied Epicurus' texts in Greek. In a letter to William Short, dated October 31, 1819, Jefferson praises Epicurus as a great giver of laws "for governing ourselves," whereas he sees Plato as "dealing out mysticisms incomprehensible to the human mind." The doctrines of Epicurus, he declares, contain everything rational in moral philosophy bequeathed by Greece and Rome. "Epictetus, indeed," Jefferson remarks, "has given us what was good of the Stoics; all beyond, of their dogmas, being hypocrisy and grimace. Their great crime was in their calumnies of Epicurus and misrepresentations of his doctrines; in which we lament to see the candid character of Cicero engaging as an accomplice." Jefferson's political thinking, there can be no doubt, reveals Epicurean tendencies. Surely, his famous declaration "I have sworn upon the altar of God eternal hostility against every form of tyranny over the mind of man" expresses feelings that Epicurus himself, as one of mankind's earliest individualists, held to with undiminishing insistence and courage.

Although Epicureanism has not enjoyed outright favor from 1800 till the present day, a number of scholars have persevered in re-evaluating Epicurus' significance in the history of ideas. Friedrich Albert Lange's *The History of Materialism* (1865) is a German scholar's attempt to do belated justice not only to Epicurus but to other philosophers carrying on his beliefs. William Wallace's *Epicureanism,* which appeared in England in 1880, is a notable example of a full-length study of Epicurus' thought that shuns the partisanship which has often marred other assessments. Another work of immense significance, as timely today as it was in 1887 when it appeared in Germany (unfortunately it is now out of print), is *Epicurea,* edited by H. Usener. Without exaggeration this volume, containing Diogenes Laertius' *Life of Epicurus,* Epicurus' three *Letters,* the *Principal Doctrines,* and a large collection of fragments and *testimonia,* is a monumental work. It has been described as the "fruit of enviable erudition, diligence, and endurance, valuable as a model for other studies." [54] Graziano Arrighetti's *Epicuro, Opere, Introduzione, testo, critico, traduzione e note,* published in Italy in 1960, is now considered the most complete edition of Epicurus; it contains fragments which had not been deciphered in Usener's time. For modern readers of English, there have appeared competent translations of Epicurus: those by Cyril Bailey in 1926, by George K. Strodach in 1963, and by Russel M. Geer in 1964.

Finally, modern scholars who have made critical analyses, both general and specialized, of Epicurus' thought are Charlampos Theodōridēs in Greece, A.-J. Festugière in France, Ettore Bignone in Italy, Cyril Bailey and Benjamin Farrington in England, and Norman W. DeWitt in the United States. Of these, Theodōridēs, Farrington, and DeWitt are the most alert and enthusiastic scholars, without whose contributions Epicurean studies would today be languishing. Students of Epicureanism will revel in the inspiration which they communicate, and will find in them refreshing sources of vigor and insight, excellencies not always characteristic of classical scholarship. Far from being apologists for or even mere defenders of Epicurus, these scholars carry on the tradition of dissent; acting as great righters, they combine an objectivity and a delicate understanding of Epicureanism that lend to their writings the humanizing qualities which must ultimately comprise the criteria for judging genuine, life-giving scholarship. They show convincingly that to Epicurus the gods, in the words of Walter Savage Landor (1775–1864)—himself a lover of classical learning, an opponent of metaphysicians, priests, and kings, and an admirer of Epicurus—the gods gave "more than Epicurus could find among the gods": "a calm conscience, a spirit averse to disputation, and a friend to enjoy his garden with him uninterrupted; a friend even dearer than solitude." [55]

Abbreviations

(B)   Translated by Cyril Bailey, *Epicurus: The Extant Remains with Short Critical Apparatus, Translation and Notes* (Oxford: Clarendon Press, 1926).

De Fin.   Cicero, *De Finibus Bonorum et Malorum* [Loeb Classical Library], trans. H. Rackham (Cambridge: Harvard University Press, 1931).

D.L.   *Diogenes Laertius, Lives of Eminent Philosophers* [Loeb Classical Library], trans. R. D. Hicks. 2 vols. (Cambridge: Harvard University Press, 1925).

(G)   Translated by Russel M. Geer, *The Letters, Principal Doctrines, and Vatican Sayings of Epicurus* (Indianapolis: Bobbs-Merrill Co., 1964).

Herod. *Letter to Herodotus.*

Men.   *Letter to Menoeceus.*

P.D.   *Principal Doctrines.*

Pyth.   *Letter to Pythocles.*

(S)   Translated by George K. Strodach, *The Philosophy of Epicurus* (Evanston, Ill.: Northwestern University Press, 1963).

V.S.   *The Vatican Sayings.*

Notes and References

Chapter One

1. *Enarrationes in Psalmos,* Ps. 124(5).
2. *D.L.* X. 3–7.
3. Walter Nigg, *The Heretics,* ed. and trans. Richard and Clara Winston (New York, 1962), p. 10.
4. *D.L.* X. 9–10.
5. William Wallace, *Epicureanism* (London, 1880), p. 24.
6. Sextus Empiricus, *Adv. math.* x. 18.
7. A.-J. Festugière, O.P., *Epicurus and His Gods* (Oxford, England, 1955), p. 21; Norman W. DeWitt, *Epicurus and His Philosophy* (Minneapolis, 1954), p. 55.
8. *Epicurus and His Philosophy,* p. 58.
9. *D.L.* IX. 64.
10. *Ibid.* IX. 61–67.
11. *Ibid.* X. 8.
12. *Ibid.* X. 7–8; quoted in *Epicurus and His Philosophy,* p. 63.
13. *Men.* 122 (G).
14. *P.D.* XXVIII (G).
15. John Milton, *Paradise Regained,* IV. 240–41.
16. *D.L.* X. 2.
17. *Epistle* I. iv. 16.
18. *D.L.* X. 11.
19. See Norman W. DeWitt, "Organization and Procedure in Epicurean Groups," *Classical Philology,* XXXI (1936), 205–11. See also *Epicurus and His Philosophy,* pp. 93 ff.
20. III. 9–13. All quotations are from *T. Lucreti Cari De Rerum Natura Libri Sex,* trans. H. A. J. Munro (London, 1920 [1864]).
21. *D.L.* X. 22.
22. *Ibid.* X. 20.
23. *Ibid.* X. 17–18; *V.S.* LV (G).

Chapter Two

1. Collier Books, 1954, pp. 18–19.
2. *The Origins of Scientific Thought* (Chicago, 1961), p. 24.

3. George Sarton, *A History of Science* (Cambridge, Mass., 1952), I, 177.

4. Aetios i. 3, 4.

5. Eduard Zeller, *Outlines of the History of Greek Philosophy* (New York, 1957), p. 46.

6. *D.L.* IX. 3.

7. Frag. 44. The numbering and the translation of the fragments of Heraclitus, Parmenides, Empedocles, and Anaxagoras are from John Burnet, *Early Greek Philosophy*, 4th ed. (New York, 1963 [1930]).

8. Frag. 20.

9. *D.L.* IX. 8.

10. Frags. 81, 41–42, 45, 36.

11. Frag. 1.

12. Sambursky, pp. 31, 34.

13. Frag. 17.

14. Frag. 11.

15. Burnet, p. 267.

16. Sambursky, p. 129.

17. Frag. 118. The numbering and the translation of the fragments of Democritus and Leucippus are from Kathleen Freeman, *Ancilla to the Pre-Socratic Philosophers* (Cambridge, Mass., 1956).

18. Burnet, p. 330, n. 2.

19. Cyril Bailey, *The Greek Atomists and Epicurus* (New York, 1964 [1928]), p. 69.

20. *D.L.* IX. 31.

21. Frag. 2.

22. *D.L.* IX. 36, 40.

23. Simplicius, in Aristotle's *de Caelo*, A. 10. 279.

24. Frag. 11.

25. Frag. 117.

26. Frags. 46, 59, 80, 89, 145, 169, 55.

27. Frags. 181, 119, 114, 191, 194, 230, 99.

28. Frags. 294, 286, 214.

29. Frags. 273, 276.

30. Frags. 297, 191.

31. *On the Nature of the Gods.* I. 120. All quotations are from *Cicero: De Natura Deorum and Academica* [Loeb Classical Library], trans. H. Rackham (London, 1933).

32. *Herod.* 40 (S); 41a (G).

33. *Ibid.* 39 (S).

34. II. 75–79.

35. I. 215–16.

36. *Herod.* 56b (G).

37. Wallace, p. 175.

38. I. 451–53.
39. *Herod.* 56a (G).
40. *Ibid.* 42b (G).
41. II. 216–93.
42. *Herod.* 60 (G).
43. II. 221–24.
44. *The Greek Atomists and Epicurus,* p. 333.
45. II. 95–99.
46. II. 304–10, 312–13, 317–32.
47. *The Greek Atomists and Epicurus,* p. 320.
48. *About the Ends of Goods and Evils.* I. vi. 19, 20.
49. George K. Strodach, *The Philosophy of Epicurus* (Evanston, Ill., 1963), p. 25.
50. *A History of Western Philosophy* (New York, 1945), p. 247.
51. *The Greek Atomists and Epicurus,* p. 338.
52. II. 277–80.
53. *V.S.* XVII (B).
54. II. 284–93.
55. *D.L.* IX. 61.
56. *Ibid.* X. 32.
57. *Herod.* 39 (S).
58. *P.D.* XXIV (B).
59. *Herod.* 49 (B).
60. Kathleen Freeman, *The Pre-Socratic Philosophers,* 2nd ed. (Oxford, England, 1959), p. 311.
61. *Herod.* 47 (B).
62. IV. 56, 58, 60–61.
63. *Herod.* 47, 48 (B).
64. *Ibid.* 52b, 53a (G).
65. *D.L.* X. 33.
66. *The Greek Atomists and Epicurus,* p. 247.
67. *Herod.* 51 (B).
68. *D.L.* X. 34.
69. IV. 354–59.
70. *D.L.* X. 34.
71. *Epicurus and His Philosophy,* p. 152.
72. *The Greek Atomists and Epicurus,* p. 250.
73. W. T. Jones, *A History of Western Philosophy* (New York, 1945), I, 90–91.
74. Russell, pp. 67, 73.
75. The phrase is from Basil Willey, *The Seventeenth-Century Background* (Garden City, N. Y., 1955), p. 15.
76. Strodach, p. 12.
77. I. Thess. 5:8.

78. Russell, p. 72.
79. *P.D.* XI (G).
80. See *Arion*, III, No. 3 (Autumn 1964), 112–19.
81. *V.S.* LXXVII (B).

Chapter Three

1. V. 206–9.
2. V. 251–52.
3. V. 305–10, 313–15.
4. *The Greek Atomists and Epicurus*, p. 359.
5. *About the Ends of Goods and Evils.* I. VII. 22.
6. Philip H. De Lacy, "The Epicurean Analysis of Language," *American Journal of Philology*, LX (1939), 85–92.
7. *D.L.* X. 120.
8. *Herod.* 45 (B).
9. *Pyth.* 88 (S).
10. *Ibid.* 89 (S).
11. *Herod.* 74 (B).
12. V. 443–48.
13. V. 495–508.
14. I. 1021–1037.
15. II. 1116–1117, 1131–1132.
16. II. 1144–1145.
17. II. 1153–54, 1156, 1173–74.
18. *Herod.* 75 (B).
19. V. 780–81.
20. V. 788–94.
21. V. 871–77.
22. V. 927–30.
23. V. 960–61.
24. V. 999–1001.
25. V. 1010.
26. *Herod.* 75 (S).
27. See Strodach, p. 233, n. 23.
28. *Herod.* 76 (S).
29. V. 1120–30.
30. V. 1370–71.
31. V. 1384–87.
32. V. 1397–1404.
33. V. 1432–35.
34. V. 1439, 1448–53.
35. V. 1455–57.
36. *Herod.* 78 (S).
37. *Pyth.* 86 (S).

38. *Ibid.* (S).
39. *Herod.* 80 (S).
40. *Pyth.* 97 (G).
41. *Ibid.* 90 (S).
42. *Ibid.* 91 (S).
43. V. 566–68.
44. *Pyth.* 92, 93 (S).
45. *Ibid.* 95 (S).
46. *Ibid.* 98 (S).
47. *Ibid.* 100 (S).
48. *Ibid.* 103, 104 (S).
49. VI. 417–20.
50. *Pyth.* 104 (S).
51. *Ibid.* 105 (S).
52. *Ibid.* 108 (S).
53. VI. 519–26.
54. *Pyth.* 110 (S).
55. *Ibid.* 111 (S).
56. *Ibid.* 112 (S).
57. *Ibid.* 114 (S).
58. *Ibid.* 115 (S).
59. Strodach, p. 49.
60. *Pyth.* 87 (S).
61. *Ibid.* 93 (S).
62. *Ibid.* 98 (S).
63. *Ibid.* 104 (S).
64. *Ibid.* 113 (S).
65. *Ibid.* 114 (S).
66. *Herod.* 82 (S).

Chapter Four

1. Alain Hus, *Greek and Roman Religion,* trans. S. J. Tester (New York, 1962), p. 75.
2. I. 68–71.
3. Gilbert Murray, *Five Stages of Greek Religion,* 3rd ed. (New York, 1951), p. 125.
4. *Men.* 132–34 (B).
5. *Ibid.* 135 (B).
6. A. H. Armstrong, *An Introduction to Ancient Philosophy,* 3rd ed. (London, 1957), p. 130.
7. *Epinomis,* 982c–983b. The quotation is from *Plato: Philebus and Epinomis,* trans. A. E. Taylor (London, 1956).
8. *Herod.* 76–77 (B).
9. *Pyth.* 86 (B).

10. *Men.* 134, 135 (B).
11. *Herod.* 81 (B).
12. *Remains Assigned to Certain Books.* III. 3 (B).
13. V. 1198–1203.
14. *Men.* 123–24 (B).
15. V. 73–75.
16. I. xvi. 42.
17. I. xvii. 44.
18. V. 148–52.
19. V. 1172–1182.
20. I. xviii. 47–49.
21. I. xix. 50.
22. *Epicurus and His Philosophy,* p. 274.
23. *The Greek Atomists and Epicurus,* p. 454.
24. III. 19–22.
25. I. xix. 51.
26. Strodach, p. 51; I. xx. 56.
27. Quoted in *The Greek Atomists and Epicurus,* p. 480.
28. *Fragments from Uncertain Sources.* 58 (B).
29. V. 165–73.
30. *Fragments from Uncertain Sources.* 57 (B); see *The Greek Atomists and Epicurus,* p. 479.
31. I. xx. 54.
32. Wallace, p. 108.
33. I. xix. 51, xx. 52.
34. *V.S.* XXXI (G).
35. Quoted in and trans. by Murray, p. 163. My italics.
36. *V.S.* XIV, XXX (B).
37. *Fragments from Uncertain Sources.* 82 (B).
38. *P.D.* II (B).
39. *Letters to Unknown Recipients.* 50 (B).
40. III. 37–40.
41. *Men.* 124–27 (B).
42. III. 838–42.
43. III. 922, 964–65, 1023.
44. III. 980–1022.
45. III. 1092–94.
46. "Eumenes." XVI. 2. The quotation is from *Plutarch's Lives,* VIII [Loeb Classical Library], trans. Bernadotte Perrin (London, 1914).
47. Murray, p. 4.
48. William R. Inge, *Christian Mysticism,* 8th ed. (London, 1948), p. 5. Italics are the author's.
49. *Theaetetus.* 176b.

50. I. viii. 18.

51. Quoted in Benjamin Farrington, *Science and Politics in the Ancient World* (London, 1939), p. 156.

52. I. xliii. 121.

53. "Alexander the False Prophet," 17, 22, 23, 24. All quotations are from *Lucian*, IV [Loeb Classical Library], trans. A. H. Harmon (London, 1913).

54. *Ibid.* 25.

55. *Ibid.* 47.

56. André Bonnard, *Greek Civilization, III: From Euripides to Alexandria,* trans. R. C. Knight (New York, 1961), 280.

57. J. William, *Diogenis Oenoandensis Fragmenta* (Leipzig, 1907), II, Col. 2, 7, 5.

Chapter Five

1. Book XI. All quotations are from Homer, *The Odyssey,* trans. S. H. Butcher and A. Lang (New York, 1950).

2. *Ibid.*

3. Erwin Rohde, *Psyche,* trans. N. B. Hillis (London, 1925), p. 55.

4. Martin P. Nilsson, *A History of Greek Religion,* trans. F. J. Fielden (Oxford, England, 1949), p. 139.

5. *Phaedo,* 79d.

6. *Phaedrus,* 245e–46a.

7. *Phaedo,* 70a.

8. Rohde, p. 472.

9. *Phaedo,* 81a.

10. *Herod.* 67 (B).

11. *Ibid.* 63 (B).

12. III. 396–99.

13. III. 141–44.

14. III. 153–56.

15. III. 162–64.

16. III. 170–74.

17. *The Greek Atomists and Epicurus,* p. 390.

18. *Herod.* 63a (B).

19. Aetios. iv. 3. 11.

20. III. 246–51.

21. *Herod.* 64 (B).

22. III. 325–30.

23. *Herod.* 64 (B).

24. *Ibid.* 65 (B).

25. *Ibid.* 65–66 (B).

26. III. 417–829. For the rest of this chapter all quotations from Lucretius are from these proofs.

27. Herodotus. III. 134.3.

28. Murray, p. 154.

29. *Ibid.*, p. 147.

30. Farrington, p. 145.

31. Quoted in R. M. Wenley, *Stoicism and Its Influence* (Boston, 1924), p. 93.

Chapter Six

1. F. W. Bussell, "Happiness (Greek and Roman)," *Encyclopaedia of Religion and Ethics*, ed. James Hastings (Edinburgh, 1913), VI, 513.

2. *P.D.* V (B).

3. Leon Robin, *Greek Thought and the Origins of the Scientific Spirit*, trans. M. R. Dobie (New York, 1928), p. 340.

4. *P.D.* XV (B).

5. *P.D.* XXII (B).

6. *Remains Assigned to Certain Books.* VI. 10 (B).

7. *The Greek Atomists and Epicurus*, p. 483.

8. IV. 482–85.

9. I. xix. 64.

10. I. xxi. 72.

11. *D.L.* II. 75.

12. George Santayana, "Lucretius," *Three Philosophical Poets* (New York, 1954 [1910]), p. 33.

13. *D.L.* X. 137.

14. Strodach, p. 227, n. 44.

15. Wallace, p. 151.

16. *V.S.* XI (B).

17. *P.D.* XIX (B).

18. *Ibid.* XXI (B).

19. *V.S.* LIX (B).

20. *Fragments from Uncertain Sources.* 59 (B).

21. *Remains Assigned to Certain Books.* VI. 11 (B).

22. *P.D.* XX (B).

23. Sextus Empiricus, *Adv. math.* xi. 169.

24. *About the Ends of Goods and Evils.* I. x. 33.

25. *P.D.* III (B).

26. *V.S.* IV (B).

27. *Men.* 129–30 (B).

28. *V.S.* XXI (B).

29. *Remains Assigned to Certain Books.* V. 8 (B).

30. *Fragments from Uncertain Sources.* 74 (B).

31. *V.S.* LXIII (B).

32. *Ibid.* LXVIII (B).

33. *Ibid.* LXIX (B).
34. *Men.* 130–31 (B).
35. *About the Ends of Goods and Evils.* I. xxi. 71–72.
36. *Fragments from Uncertain Sources.* 54 (B).
37. *Ibid.* 85.
38. II. 1–21.
39. *P.D.* XIV (B).
40. *Ibid.* XXXIX (B).
41. R. D. Hicks, *Stoic and Epicurean* (New York, 1962), pp. 166–67.
42. *D.L.* X. 118.
43. *Fragments from Uncertain Sources.* 81 (B).
44. *P.D.* XXXIII (B).
45. *Ibid.* XL (B).
46. *V.S.* IX (B).
47. *Ibid.* LXVII (B).
48. *Letters to Unknown Recipients.* 48 (B).
49. *V.S.* XLIV (B).
50. W. Windelband, *History of Ancient Philosophy,* trans. H. E. Cushman (New York, 1956), p. 324.
51. Zeller, p. 260.
52. John Masson, *Lucretius: Epicurean and Poet* (New York, 1907), I, 345.
53. Festugière, p. xi.
54. VI. 24–26.

Chapter Seven

1. Quoted in "On Having Many Friends," *Plutarch's Moralia* [Loeb Classical Library], trans. Frank C. Babbitt (Cambridge, Mass., 1928), 93.C.1.
2. *D. H. Lawrence: A Composite Biography,* ed. Edward Nehls (Madison, Wisc., 1957), I, 501.
3. *V.S.* LII (B).
4. Xenophon, *Oeconomicus,* VII. 30–32.
5. Theognis, 237. See G. Lowes Dickinson, *The Greek View of Life* (London, 1957 [1896]), pp. 186–87.
6. 1155a/3–5. Quotations are from *The Basic Works of Aristotle,* ed. Richard McKeon (New York, 1941). The translation is by W. D. Ross.
7. W. M. Rankin, "Friendship," *Encyclopaedia of Religion and Ethics,* VI, 131.
8. Adolf von Harnack, *The Mission and Expansion of Christianity,* ed. and trans. James Moffatt (New York, 1962), p. 25.
9. *D.L.* VIII. 23–24.
10. *Ibid.* VIII. 23.

11. *Ibid.* VIII. 33.

12. *Ibid.* VIII. 10.

13. *Symposium,* 211b–c.

14. John Ferguson, *Moral Values in the Ancient World* (London, 1958), p. 67.

15. IX. 1170a.

16. VIII. 1157b.

17. "On Having Many Friends," 93.C.2.

18. *About the Ends of Goods and Evils.* I. xx. 65.

19. *V.S.* LXXVIII (G).

20. *D.L.* X. 11.

21. Ferguson, p. 75.

22. *About the Ends of Goods and Evils.* II. xxi. 67–68.

23. *V.S.* LX (G).

24. *P.D.* III (G).

25. *V.S.* XLVIII (G).

26. *P.D.* XXVII (G).

27. *V.S.* XXVIII (B).

28. *P.D.* XXVIII (G).

29. *V.S.* XXIII (G).

30. *V.S.* XXXIV (G).

31. *V.S.* LVI–LVII (B).

32. *V.S.* XLIII (G).

33. *About the Ends of Goods and Evils.* I. xx. 65.

34. *Letters to Individuals.* To Pythocles. 34 (B).

35. *Letters to Uncertain Persons.* To Leontion. 32 (B).

36. *Letters to Individuals.* To Themista. 25 (B).

37. *Letters to Unknown Recipients.* 38 (B).

38. *V.S.* XXXII (B).

39. *Letters to Individuals.* To Colotes.

40. *P.D.* VIII (B).

41. *P.D.* XVIII (G).

42. See Chap. 1, n. 12.

43. H. D. F. Kitto, *The Greeks* (Baltimore, 1957), p. 220. See also Hans Licht, "Male Homosexuality," *Sexual Life in Ancient Greece* (New York, 1963 [1932]), pp. 411–98.

44. *V.S.* LXXX (B).

45. *Ibid.* XVII (B).

46. *Ibid.* LI (B).

47. IV. 1037–1287.

48. IV. 1115–20.

49. *Remains Assigned to Certain Books.* V. 8.

50. W. W. Tarn, *Hellenistic Civilisation,* 2nd ed. (London, 1930), p. 294.

51. Charlampos Theodōridē, *Epicurus: The Real Face of the Ancient World* (Athens, 1954), p. 86. My translation.
52. Murray, p. 103.

Chapter Eight

1. George S. Brett, *A History of Psychology* (London, 1921), II. 218; *Epicurus and His Philosophy*, p. 8.
2. *D.L.* X. 9.
3. Friedrich A. Lange, *The History of Materialism*, 3rd ed. (New York, 1925), I, 126.
4. "Cato Major," III. 7; IV. 1, 2; XVI. 5, in *Plutarch's Lives*, II [Loeb Classical Library], trans. Bernadotte Perrin (London, 1914).
5. *Ibid.* XII. 4, 5; XVI. 2.
6. *Ibid.* XXII. 2.
7. *Ibid.* XXII. 4.
8. *The Cambridge Ancient History*, ed. S. A. Cook and others (New York, 1930), VIII, 398.
9. *Ibid.*, VIII, 463.
10. "Tusculan Disputations," IV. iii. 6, in *Cicero: Tusculan Disputations* [Loeb Classical Library], trans. J. E. King (Cambridge, Mass., 1927).
11. "Caius Marius," XLIII. 5; XLIV. 6, in *Plutarch's Lives*, IX [Loeb Classical Library], trans. Bernadotte Perrin (London, 1914).
12. "Sulla," XXXI, in *Plutarch's Lives*, IV [Loeb Classical Library], trans. Bernadotte Perrin (London, 1914).
13. *Ibid.* XXXI. 4.
14. John W. Duff, *A Literary History of Rome*, 3rd ed. (London, 1953), p. 221.
15. *About the Ends of Goods and Evils.* II. xxxv. 119.
16. *Tusc. Disp.* I. i. 2.
17. *Cicero's Three Books of Offices, or Moral Duties*, trans. Cyrus R. Edmonds (New York, 1897), Book III. Chap. 33.
18. *Tusc. Disp.* V. xxvii. 78.
19. "In Pisonem," X. 22; XII. 27; XXV; XXVII, 66, 67, in *Cicero: The Speeches* [Loeb Classical Library], trans. N. H. Watts (London, 1931).
20. *Ibid.* XXVIII. 68.
21. *Ibid.* XXVIII. 69.
22. "Fragment of a Letter to a Priest," 301 C–D, in *The Works of the Emperor Julian* [Loeb Classical Library], trans. Wilmer C. Wright (Cambridge, Mass., 1913).
23. *Epistle* 118.21.
24. *On Prescription Against Heretics*, Chap. 7.
25. Confession VII. 21, in *St. Augustine's Confessions*, I [Loeb

Classical Library], trans. William Watts (Cambridge, Mass., 1912).

26. *The Miscellanies,* Vol. II, Book VII, Chap. 3.

27. Book III, Chap. 17.

28. Christopher Dawson, *Religion and the Rise of Western Culture* (New York, 1950), p. 33.

29. *The Comedy of Dante Alighieri,* trans. Dorothy L. Sayers (Baltimore, 1949), Canto IX. 109–11; Canto IX. 118–21; Canto X. 10.

30. *St. Augustine's Confessions,* Vol. I, Book VI, Chap. 16.

31. I Peter 2:9.

32. Luke 12:32.

33. Minneapolis, 1959, p. 179.

34. *Ibid.,* p. v.

35. Lange, I, 255.

36. Meyrick Carré, *Phases of Thought in England* (Oxford, England, 1949), p. 224.

37. Quoted in Charles T. Harrison, "The Ancient Atomists and English Literature of the Seventeenth Century," *Harvard Studies in Classical Philology,* XLV (1934), 4.

38. *The Works of Sir Thomas Browne,* ed. Geoffrey Keynes (Chicago, 1964). See "Pseudodoxia Epidemica," in Vol. II, Book VII, Chap. 17, Sect. 8.

39. Harrison, p. 21.

40. Thomas F. Mayo, *Epicurus in England (1650–1725)* (Dallas, 1934), pp. 38, 39.

41. Ralph Cudworth, *The True Intellectual System of the Universe, I* (London, 1678), 170.

42. "John Bramhall," in T. S. Eliot, *Selected Essays* (New York, 1960), p. 312.

43. Mayo, p. 115.

44. Frederick J. E. Woodbridge, "Hobbes," *Encyclopaedia of Religion and Ethics,* VI, 729.

45. Joseph Glanvill, *The Vanity of Dogmatizing* (New York, 1931), p. 146.

46. Abraham Cowley, *Essays, Plays and Sundry Verses,* ed. A. R. Waller (New York, 1906), p. 398.

47. *A Collection of Several Philosophical Writings of Henry More,* 4th ed. (London, 1712), p. 85.

48. Quoted in George A. Panichas, "The Greek Spirit and the Mysticism of Henry More," *The Greek Orthodox Theological Review,* II (Christmas Issue, 1956), 19.

49. George D. Hadzsits, *Lucretius and His Influence* (New York, 1963), p. 323.

50. Lange, II, 17.

51. Quoted in Mayo, p. 223.

52. Carré, p. 379.
53. *Epicurus and His Philosophy*, p. 357.
54. Theodōridē, p. 209.
55. Walter Savage Landor, *Imaginary Conversations* (London, 1891), I, 280, 281.

Selected Bibliography

(This bibliography is confined only to studies which can be of most help in introducing a reader to Epicurus' philosophy. With the exception of some of the texts and translations, all works mentioned are in English. For a specialized bibliography, one should consult Philip De Lacy's "Some Recent Publications on Epicurus and Epicureanism [1937–1954]," *Classical Weekly*, XLVIII [1954–55], 169–77.)

PRIMARY SOURCES
(Texts and Translations)

Bailey, Cyril. *Epicurus: The Extant Remains with Short Critical Apparatus, Translation and Notes.* Oxford: Clarendon Press, 1926. Containing the Greek text and the English translation of the three *Letters,* the *Principal Doctrines,* Diogenes Laertius' "The Life of Epicurus," the *Vatican Sayings,* and many fragments, with Introduction and Commentary, this volume occupies a place of lasting importance in the field of Epicurean studies.

Diano, C. *Epicuri Ethica.* Florence: Sansoni, 1946. This is a collection of Epicurus' Greek texts on ethics and has a Latin commentary and indexes.

Geer, Russel M., trans. *Epicurus: Letters, Principal Doctrines, and Vatican Sayings.* Indianapolis: Bobbs-Merrill, 1964. This volume contains a brief section from "The Life of Epicurus" by Diogenes Laertius; the three *Letters;* and the *Principal Doctrines.* Geer has added his own titles and summaries to the *Letters.* The Introduction is a model of concision and perceptiveness. Longer notes and commentary are found in the Appendix. Geer's English translation is very readable, and the book as a whole is of value both to classicists and general readers.

Hicks, R. D. *Diogenes Laertius: Lives of Eminent Philosophers, with an English Translation* [Loeb Classical Library]. 2 vols. Cambridge: Harvard University Press, 1925. Book X, "The Life of Epicurus," containing the three *Letters* and the *Principal Doctrines,* is found in the second volume. The English translation faces the Greek text. This is an essential book for biographical and doctrinal details of Epicurus' life and teachings. The Introduction to the first volume contains information on the manuscript tradition and on early printed editions.

Leonard, William E., and Stanley Barney Smith, eds. *T. Lucreti Cari. De Rerum Natura. Libri Sex.* Madison, Wisc.: University of Wisconsin Press, 1942. This superb volume contains the Latin text and commentary, as well as a general introduction on "Lucretius: The Man, the Poet, and the Times." The commentary, which is preceded by a separate introduction, is a source book of information not only on Lucretius but also on Epicurus.

Strodach, George K. *The Philosophy of Epicurus.* Evanston, Ill.: Northwestern University Press, 1963. This is a modern, competent, and scrupulously annotated translation which includes excerpts from "The Life of Epicurus" by Diogenes Laertius; the three *Letters;* the *Principal Doctrines;* and the *Vatican Collection of Aphorisms,* of which only a selection of the eighty-one sayings is presented. Parallel passages from Lucretius' *On the Nature of Things,* translated by Strodach, are also included. A long and lively introductory essay on ancient materialism is an added feature of this book.

Usener, H. *Epicurea.* Leipzig: B. G. Teubneri, 1887. A pioneering and basic work, this volume contains all of Epicurus' works and writings extant in 1887, as well as *testimonia* from later Epicurean writers. A Latin commentary is included.

Von der Muehll, P. *Epicuri epistulae tres et ratae sententiae e Laertio Diogene servatae; accedit Gnomologium Epicureum vaticanum.* Leipzig: B. G. Teubneri, 1922. Though this small book (69 pp.) omits the fragments, it contains the best Greek text of the three *Letters,* the *Principal Doctrines,* and the *Vatican Collection.*

William, J., ed. *Diogenis Oenoandensis fragmenta.* Leipzig: B. G. Teubneri, 1907. This edition makes available the fragments of letters and aphorisms of Diogenes of Oenoanda. An introduction and notes in Latin are included.

SECONDARY SOURCES

Bailey, Cyril. *The Greek Atomists and Epicurus.* New York: Russell and Russell, 1964 [1928]. An eminently readable study of the development of Greek atomism, it contains sections on "The Antecedents of Atomism," on Leucippus, and on Democritus. The major part is devoted to Epicurus' philosophical system.

Barclay, William. "Hellenistic Thought in New Testament Times. The Way of Tranquillity. The Epicureans—I and II," *The Expository Times,* LXXII, 78–81; 101–4. These two essays should be required reading, as they contain perhaps the best written and most succinct explication of Epicurus' life and thought to have appeared in recent years.

Bonnard, André. *Greek Civilization. From Euripides to Alexandria.* III. New York: Macmillan, 1957–61. The final chapter of this famous three-volume work concludes, appropriately, with an evocative chapter on "Epicurus and the Salvation of Man."

Brink, K. O. "Epicurus," *The Oxford Classical Dictionary,* ed. M. Cary, and others. Oxford: Clarendon Press, 1949, pp. 324–25. As a summary of Epicurus' thought, this article is worthwhile.

De Lacy, Philip H. "The Epicurean Analysis of Language," *American Journal of Philology,* LX (1939), 85–92. This essay relates to the Epicurean preference for simple prose and disdain for rhetoric and poetry.

De Santillana, Giorgio. *The Origins of Scientific Thought, from Anaximander to Proclus, 600 B. C. to 300 A. D.* Chicago: University of Chicago Press, 1961. This volume provides background reading. The chapter on "Atoms and the Void" is of especial interest for its discussion of Democritus.

DeWitt, Norman J. "Epicurus Relocated," *Arion,* III (Autumn 1964), 113–19. Written as a review of Strodach's translation, this stimulating article contains insights into Epicurus' opposition to "organization theory."

DeWitt, Norman W. *Epicurus and His Philosophy.* Minneapolis: University of Minnesota Press, 1954. Written by one of Epicurus' most indefatigable defenders, this volume gives an account of Epicurus' life, interprets his doctrines, and discusses Epicureanism as a point of transition from ancient Greek philosophy to Christianity. Intent on "rescuing Epicurus from the injustice of centuries," DeWitt rebuts the slanders and fallacies surrounding Epicurus and argues with and rebukes other scholars and translators. Although panegyrical, it is a brave and an outstanding scholarly contribution.

DeWitt, Norman W. *St. Paul and Epicurus.* Minneapolis: University of Minnesota Press, 1954. A sequel to the author's *Epicurus and His Philosophy,* this work attempts to show how Epicureanism acted "as a bridge of transition from Greek philosophy to the Christian religion," and how St. Paul's writings were influenced, directly or indirectly, by Epicurean teachings. As usual, DeWitt writes persuasively.

Elder, J. P. Review of Norman W. DeWitt, *Epicurus and His Philosophy. American Journal of Philology,* LXXVII (1956), 75–84. Incisive, if at times condescending, this review serves as a corrective to DeWitt's "apostolic fervor," pointing out both strengths and weaknesses of DeWitt's approach.

Farrington, Benjamin. *Science and Politics in the Ancient World.* London: G. Allen & Unwin, 1939. This provocative book vigorously asserts the values of Epicurus as a champion of science and enlightenment, opposed to the rigidity and the totalitarian orientation of Plato. For any student of Epicureanism this volume is indispensable—and unforgettable for the impact it makes.

Ferguson, John. *Moral Values in the Ancient World.* London: Methuen & Co., 1958. This exceptionally able study includes chapters on "Friendship," "Eros," "Philanthropia," and "Agape," wherein observations on Epicurus' ideas are rewarding.

Festugière, A.-J. *Epicurus and His Gods,* trans. C. W. Chilton. Oxford: Basil Blackwell, 1955. Translated from the French, this short work brilliantly and sensitively examines Epicurus' ethical and religious doctrines, set against their historical background. The comparisons drawn between Plato and Epicurus are particularly arresting.

Fitzgerald, William H. "Pietas Epicurea," *Classical Journal,* XLVI (1951), 195–99. Upholding Epicurus' religious meaning, this essay underscores the element of reverence in his teachings.

Freeman, Kathleen. "Epicurus—A Social Experiment," *Greece and Rome,* VII (May 1938), 156–68. This article by a distinguished classical scholar and translator stresses that Epicurus' main contribution to philosophy was his theory of happiness. And the school at Athens served as his "working-model," where his followers, rejecting "the idea of service," concentrated on self-development and self-realization.

"The Garden of Epicurus." Anon. rev., *Times Literary Supplement,* April 13, 1956, pp. 213–14. A long review of Festugière's *Epicurus and His Gods,* it also serves aptly as a general statement on Epicurus' thought. It has some good insights into the theology.

Greene, William C. *Moira. Fate, Good, and Evil in Greek Thought.* New York: Harper and Row, 1963 [1944]. A work of profound learning, it is especially important in respect to the history of religious and ethical thought. Chapter XI, "Fate and Providence," contains a short discussion of Epicurus' rejection of fatalism.

Hadzsits, George D. *Lucretius and Epicureanism.* Boston: Marshall Jones Co., 1926. Although devoted to Lucretius, this book contains many references to Epicurean doctrine as a whole. The chapters dealing with the Epicurean-Lucretian reputation and influence from the time of the Roman Empire through the twentieth century are of special value.

Hall, Clayton M. "Some Epicureans at Rome," *The Classical Weekly,* XXVIII, 113–15. This article presents a useful description of important Roman Epicureans during the first century B.C.

Harrison, Charles T. "The Ancient Atomists and English Literature of the Seventeenth Century," *Harvard Studies in Classical Philology,* XLV (1934), 1–79. This is a painstaking appraisal of the influences of Epicurus' atomic theory and doctrines as a whole on English writers, translators, clergymen, and philosophers. Lucretius' significance is also brought out.

Hicks, R. D. "Epicureans," *Encyclopaedia of Religion and Ethics,* ed. James Hastings, V (Edinburgh: T. and T. Clark, 1912), 324–30. This is a thorough and informative survey article.

Hicks, R. D. *Stoic and Epicurean.* New York: Russell and Russell, 1962. Three chapters, covering over two hundred pages, are devoted to "Epicurus and Hedonism," "The Atomic Theory," and "The Epicurean Theology." The treatment of Epicurus, though cautious, is always fair-minded.

Jones, W. T. *A History of Western Philosophy.* New York: Harcourt, Brace, 1952. The first volume contains two excellently written and balanced chapters, Chap. 3, "Atomism," and Chap. 8 (especially pp. 260–66) on Epicurus.

Lange, Friedrich A. *The History of Materialism,* trans. Ernest C. Thomas with Intro. by Bertrand Russell. 3rd ed. New York: Harcourt, Brace, 1925. This celebrated volume traces the development of the philosophical concept of materialism from earliest times to the mid-nineteenth century. The part (Book I, Chap. 4) on Epicurus treats him with deep respect and appreciation.

Mair, A. W. "Epicurus," *Encyclopaedia Britannica.* Chicago: William Benton, 1963, VIII, 638–40. Clear and direct, this is as good a summary of Epicurus' philosophical system as could be desired. It also contains a useful bibliography.

Mayo, Thomas F. *Epicurus in England 1650–1725.* Dallas, Texas: Southwest Press, 1934. Excellently researched and neatly organized, this study assesses the revival, diffusion, and fairly wide acceptance of Epicurean philosophy in England.

Mins, Henry F. "Marx's Doctoral Dissertation," *Science and Society,* XII (Winter 1948), 157–69. This informative article discusses the dissertation in which Marx showed differences between the Democritean and Epicurean philosophies of nature.

Murray, Gilbert. *Five Stages of Greek Religion.* New York: Doubleday & Co., 1951. A distinguished study of various phases of ancient Greek religious thought, it contains an enlightening chapter on "The Great Schools of the Fourth Century B. C.," in which there appears a section devoted to Epicurus.

Russell, Bertrand. *A History of Western Philosophy.* New York: Simon and Schuster, 1945, pp. 240–51. Chapter XXVII of this famous volume, which seeks to "exhibit philosophy as an integral part of social and political life," contains a discussion of "The Epicureans." Russell's trenchant prose style inevitably facilitates the reader's understanding.

Sambursky, Samuel. *The Physical World of the Greeks.* New York: Collier Books, 1954. An Israeli physicist examines the ancient Greek view of the world and its relation to modern scientific method. The discussion of the atomic ideas of Leucippus, Democritus, Epicurus, and Lucretius is illuminating.

Simpson, Adelaide D. "Epicureans, Christians, Atheists in the Second Century," *Transactions and Proceedings of the American Philological Association,* LXXII (1941), 372–81. This study analyzes some of the reasons for unfavorably pairing Epicureans and Christians. It suggests that in the *Octavius* of Minucius Felix two characters, both Christians, Octavius and Minucius, were originally Epicureans. The resemblances between Epicureanism and Christianity are convincingly drawn.

Tarn, W. W. *Hellenistic Civilisation,* 3rd ed. Cleveland and New York: World Publishing Co., 1961 [1927]. Written by a great historian of antiquity, this volume covers the three centuries between the death of Alexander the Great and the establishment of the Roman Empire by Augustus. Diverse aspects of Hellenistic life and society are discussed. The final chapter on "Philosophy and Religion" is especially acute. For background reading this book is commendable.

Turner, J. Hilton. "Epicurus and Friendship," *The Classical Journal,* XLII (March 1947), 351–55. This well-argued interpretation of the meaning of friendship in Epicurean doctrines effectively defends Epicurean friendship against the charge of self-interest.

Ueberweg, Friedrich. *History of Philosophy. Vol. I: History of the Ancient and Mediaeval Philosophy,* trans. from the fourth German edition by George S. Morris, with additions by Noah Porter. New York: Charles Scribner's Sons, 1892. This monumental work, enhanced by a careful collection of authorities, bibliographies, and citations, devotes a fairly long section to Epicurus' life and doctrines. Primary and secondary Epicurean sources are quoted liberally.

Wallace, William. *Epicureanism.* London: Society for Promoting Christian Knowledge, 1880. This volume contains many refreshing insights; throughout it is sympathetic in its treatment of Epicureanism. Unfortunately this book is now out of print.

Warner, Rex. *The Greek Philosophers.* New York: New American Library, 1958. A "serviceable sketch" of Greek philosophy from the Pre-Socratics through Plotinus, this book contains a chapter on Epicurus and quotes often from Bailey's translation of the texts.

Zeller, Eduard. *Outlines of the History of Greek Philosophy*, ed. Wilhelm Nestle and trans. L. R. Palmer. 13th ed. New York: Meridian Books, 1955. This standard, systematic work, originally published in 1883, contains a survey of "Hellenistic Philosophy. The Stoa. The Later Cynicism. Epicureanism. Scepticism. Eclecticism." The part on "Pre-Socratic Philosophy" is also pertinent.

Index

Index